Love: *"It's How I Manifest"*

On Abundance, Happiness, Joy, and Peace of Mind

By Mandy Morris

Table of Contents

Introduction

I'm sitting here in my kitchen typing this to you. I expect this book, built into the next 30 days, to massively change your life. I mean, exponentially. I don't say that lightly. This book is going to be written with the purest intention I have in me to serve you. It is built around concepts and information I picked up throughout my life, observed from others, and finally applied fully in my life just about a year and a half ago. I then took these concepts and shared them. And it has been a 100% success up to this point.

I remember waking up every day crying, or near tears, not having the energy for work, in unhealthy friendships and relationships, and feeling really lost; disconnected from my spirit like there was Saran Wrap between myself and my soul. I knew it was there, but it just couldn't get through. The lack of alignment within myself was crippling. I remember the exact moment things began to shift. I was sitting in my tiny one-bedroom apartment in Florida. A few months prior, I had moved across the country for a job I didn't want but it paid well. Now I sat in my condo alone, crying. I went into the bathroom and stared at myself as tears streamed down my face. I looked and looked into my eyes trying to find someone in there. Someone I could recognize. A rush of what felt like pure loving energy came over me, and I knew what I needed to do. At that moment, I promised the world I would show up for humanity. I would do what I came here to do, and I prayed to God to just give me the direction I needed because I was too clouded to know how to get back to me, but I knew it was the solution. Man, was I in for a wild ride. It took two weeks for me to receive the subtle synchronicities that I honored, and I soon left relationships, quit my job, started traveling, and fully plunged into finding my alignment, thus leading to my purpose work.

So, what is my purpose here on this planet? To raise the world up to a love frequency. Those words may mean something different for everyone, but it will be felt the same universally. And how do I believe that can be done? By creating a ripple effect of others also finding their alignment and igniting their consciousness to find their work—to give their own gifts to the world *fearlessly*. That is why I am writing this book. That is why I have created the Authentic Life 30-Day Program. It's why I'm going to give you a free gift at the end of this introduction, to illuminate your path in the same fashion I followed and now have been blessed to tell to hundreds of others, soon thousands, and then millions and beyond.

I suggest reading one chapter a day and doing any activities I place in there at the same time that you read them. There is a lot of processing, shifting, and possible changes that will need to take place, and your subconscious mind will process best with one lesson per day. Use this book as a tool, a guide made to show you how much you are loved and how deeply important I know you are and need you to recognize. It is not by chance you're reading this. This book is built so that you no longer stray. It's built so that you get so tight-knit with your truths that life becomes this beautiful flow, and you avoid most pain naturally, simply because you are on a different frequency and can't attract disharmonies into your life.

It's important to remember your mind is an intricate piece of work. It can be a weapon, a gift, or a tool, and it is up to you how you use it to create the life you desire. I went from an extremely unfulfilling life to pure epic passion.

From jobs that I wasn't challenged in, with bosses who even wanted to fire me for lack of trying anymore, to a "born to be" entrepreneur with great success quickly.

From afraid of the unknown and paralyzed in scarcity to running wild and living in faith.

From unhealthy and empty relationships and friendships to being surrounded by the richest, loving, and most supportive people.

You'd look in my eyes and see me somewhere in there, but far away. A silent sadness that said, "I'm afraid I'm not going to make it there." There being a place of magic, opportunity, life purpose, and total epic-ness. Now, I practically jump out at you and my skin glows.

And it's not because I can afford some fancy face cream. It's because I've found how to be authentic. To my core of myself, I finally fell back in love with me. I reintroduced myself, dug deep and struck gold. And I literally know, when I'm operating in Authenticity, there's nothing I can't have, create or experience. Literally, everything I desire and write down shows up now. My gift to you is this thought: If you want to bend time to what you want to have or create in this life, of whom you desire to be for the world, simply, and difficulty, find your authentic self—the stripped-down, following intuition, believing in a mixture of magic and motion self—to get life back in alignment for you. And I swear on my life, this will unlock your wildest dreams.

I'm living proof of it. Everyone I have been blessed to touch with this full understanding has done an 180-degree turn in all areas they wanted. This. All of this . . . is because I chose Authenticity. Because when I'm authentic, I vibrate on the exact frequency so that the amount of happiness, money, growth, contribution, and love that I desire knows exactly how to find me. I'm a straight shot for what I desire because I'm not hiding under false identities and beliefs.

So, in essence, there's no confusion in the Universe.

As promised a few paragraphs ago, I want to invite you to dig deep with me, learn my processes and principles of manifestation, and I want it to be free for you. That's why I put together a FREE TRAINING called "Authentic Creation: 4 Steps I Use to Manifest Anything I Want." This training has 75 minutes of high energy information that you can immediately use in your life. You'll want to take notes! You can get instant access at the following website: www.manifestwithmandy.com/specialtraining. Do it before you forget!

I have a deep, genuine, and compassionate understanding and care for humans, and my life purpose is to set raise them up and set them free. But I had to first do that for myself.

With all the world changes you experience daily, weekly, annually, and even in your lifetime, you deserve to know and understand the tools to be unshakable, and unbreakable, no matter the external situations at hand. Your truest self, your authentic self, has all the answers you need already . . .

I wish you all the blessings on this journey. I think you are incredible, and the world, your family, your friends, clients, enemies, and everyone in the future you're going to touch need you.

And in case no one has told you today,

I love you.

Chapter 1: Living Consciously

Here we are: The first step to finding (well, *re-finding)* your authentic self.

I remember when I was in my late teens to early twenties, I was going through this really big block in being able to express myself and feel safe in showing my feelings. It was miserable, honestly, but my belief was that if I expressed myself and the pain I was experiencing fully, I would not receive love from the people in my life. I want to gift you with this crucial tool because it will be one of the most defining factors of your life for multiple reasons. It is learning, and then continuously having, the ability to live consciously. In a nutshell, this means that when you feel off emotionally or energetically, whether you know the reason or not, that you allow for yourself to become aware of it. We aren't even getting into dealing with it yet, but just showing it some *awareness*. The absolute worst thing you can do to yourself is to bury or ignore feelings when they come up. Why? Emotions, feelings, and intuition are little compasses leading you to a fulfilling life, and to your truest version of you, where all the happiness and true desires lie. So, if you bury an emotion, a feeling or a "ping" of intuition that needed to be acknowledged, you condition yourself for a particular norm, like all things in life. The problem is, we are gifted with emotions, feelings, and intuition for a *very* important reason and purpose, and you ignoring them is like a slap in the face to the Universe. The Universe is simply a Xerox, and it's going to send you copy after copy of what it best interprets that you want.

When you cling to something or don't allow for it to flow through you, you literally cause a blockage of energy. Or when you think about or act upon something long enough you create a dense amount of energetic activity in one "spot." Or when you consistently stress, you collect energy in parts of your body, and the immune system gets weaker, or diseases eventually show up, creating a psychosomatic response.

When enough energy is put into any space, it either needs to be released or it will be made manifest as particles that are influenced by frequency (and yes, *everything* has a frequency; I think even plankton vibrate at a rate of around two cycles per second...), which start moving really fast as they begin to change into denser matter and eventually . . . matter we can see.

So... in essence, thoughts *can* become things.

Now, the next trick is knowing *what* you're thinking on a non-conscious level, and *make* those thoughts conscious, and *then*... rewire them to an autoresponder that says, "I smell bullshit; replace thought or reaction to stimuli in *this* way." But don't worry, we have a chapter on how that works later. Manipulating the gray matter in the brain is one way, mindful meditation is another, exercising can work. Me? I like to live consciously.

We sometimes think that "burying our emotions" is a good thing. When some kind of emotion comes up—grief, anger, frustration or sadness—we just push it to the side thinking, "I'll deal with this later." We bury them somewhere in our subconscious mind. Instead of embracing these emotions, we tend to negate them. Your subconscious mind, however, tends to allow things to resurface over time, but if something has been buried for long enough, it's going to come up in a weird way that at times will be difficult to even trace back. For example, in my late teens, I was in a relationship with someone whose full love I felt I didn't have. I never wanted to speak my mind and my frustrations and need for love because I didn't want him to leave or cheat on me, so I kept it to myself. Slowly, I began just hating myself; I even stopped eating because I thought maybe he didn't love me enough because I wasn't as attractive as I could be. Then I stopped making friends, thinking maybe he would love me more if he saw how dedicated I was to him and him only. It was a long and miserable relationship, and it wasn't until I honored my true feelings as they came up that I was able to begin saving myself. Imagine your boss flipping out on you at work. You suppress it, act like nothing happened. A few days later, the frustration has festered, but you've consciously forgotten all about the boss's blowout, so the frustration builds up on a more unconscious level. Then, you go home one day and flip out on something your partner did to upset you. This whole scenario stemmed from a projection your boss put onto you; you carried that energy with you subconsciously, and it resurfaced in an ugly way.

When you live consciously, you remove the need to have out-of-control experiences in life, and it allows for you to be in a state of calmness and love within yourself, thus projecting outwardly into your world and bringing you even more of it.

Learning how to embrace our emotions is a prerequisite in attaining authenticity. By being conscious of our emotions, we prevent negativity from settling inside of us. By acknowledging them, we give ourselves the power to transmute it. By holding the emotions by their horns, we take control of them instead of them taking control of us.

People who bury their emotions think that negation is the shortcut to peace of mind. Wrong! I get it—confronting emotions seems so much more painful. This is the reason why we refuse to deal with them. It's like being confronted by a dark and scary figure. We can't look at it straight in the eyes, much less embrace it. We think our best defense is to run away, but that is an impossible task when it comes to emotion. In my Authentic Manifestation 30-Day Program, I talk about how deeply emotion controls our reality, and even when we say we want things like money or relationships, we actually desire an emotional state. Realizing that emotions play a vital role in our reality helps us in knowing how to handle them more carefully.

Here are some manifestations of buried emotions:

- Waking up in a bad mood for no apparent reason
- Sudden outburst to your spouse or people you live with
- Recurring feelings of self-hate and frustration
- Feelings of deep sadness

Now, check if you are in the habit of negating emotions...

- When you say, "I'm okay. I'm fine," even if you're not feeling good about something
- When you can't say what you truly feel to a person for

fear of being rejected, ridiculed, or judged

- When you take refuge in over self-indulgence (eating, drinking, drugs) during emotional lows

- When you snap at people for the pettiest of reasons

- When you give too many excuses for the people who hurt you that you become a victim

I promise you, it's impossible to bury emotions. They can't be destroyed by negation. When you think you are burying the negative emotions, you are actually planting a seed—a seed that is then watered with negligence—and it eventually resurfaces in an ugly and unpredictable way. It must instead be processed and transmuted.

Techniques

Here are some practical techniques for consciously embracing emotion:

Start an emotion journal. Each day, journal the emotions that you've been through. This will enable you to acknowledge in writing the feelings and sentiments of the day. I write every day, sometimes multiple times a day; it really works for me to see how many different emotions I may go through and decide why I experienced the ones I did.

Transmute your emotion. When your emotion comes, go to a private place where you can be alone for a while. Close your eyes and breathe slowly. Breathe deeply. Feel life going through you until your whole body is relaxed and your mind is clear. Revisit the emotion. Elevate it until it has no more power over you. Dry that negative emotion with a visualization that makes sense for you. When I feel an emotion is stuck in me, I imagine a vacuum literally sucking the dark smoke out of whatever part of my body is feeling affected.

Do emotional checks. Set your mobile phone alarms with three-hour intervals. Once the alarm sounds off, check yourself and your emotional state. We tend to get stuck in negative cycles, so cutting into them allows for conscious awareness to be brought in. If you find you're already in an awesome state, give it some gratitude and vibe on!

Pour out to a coach or a trusted confidante. Talk to a person who you truly trust; a person who accepts and loves you for who you are. It's important that this is someone you trust entirely. Tell him or her your raw emotion. Let it out. But be careful not to turn it into a victim party. Focus on the emotion. Don't pass any judgment on the person or people who you may feel caused you that emotional harm.

Write and burn. Write that emotion and the issues related to it on paper. Read it out loud. Then, burn it.

Watch it turn to ashes. This ritual helps in creating closure to an emotional burden.

Closing Reflections

We embrace not only the negative emotions, but the positive as well. There are people who negate positive and happy emotions. These are the people who frown when they should be smiling; who cry when they should be celebrating; who stoop down when they should be walking with their chins up. Some people are afraid to be happy.

Being authentic means embracing our vulnerability. Emotions are neither good nor bad. It is what it is. The 72,000 emotional receptacles all over our bodies dictate how we feel or react in varying life situations. We can only control our reactions to them.

Consciously embrace your emotions and start living an authentic life.

Prayer to the Universe

Grant me the courage to face and embrace my emotions. Emotions are gifts. They manifest my power to feel and create. May I see emotions not as frightening giants that are bent on stepping on me but as opportunities for growth, self-knowledge, and expansion.

Chapter 2: What About You Is Not You

Hey, you! Good morning, afternoon, or evening, depending on when you decide to pick back up on the second day of our journey. So today, I want to warn you . . . it's about to get *real*.

I love talking about the concepts we are going to explore in this chapter, but it's likely going to blow your mind.

First, let me explain why I believe this concept is so crucial to a life well-lived. Since we were children, we have been programmed by our parents, people in authority and other influencers to think and believe in certain ways. This is the reason why I say, "What about you is not you?" In this session, I want to help you make an inventory of your belief systems so you can discern those who serve you well and those who don't. Then, it is up to your own free will to begin the process of letting go of what isn't yours to keep. There was a time in my life where I operated mainly out of guilt—on a very conscious and subconscious level. People even learned how to use that trait against me to get what they wanted and, sometimes, they didn't even consciously understand they were doing it. I remember I stayed in poor friendships and relationships, I would work extra hours to the point of getting sick, and I would overextend myself in most areas. All because I was deeply wired to be guilt-driven. When I looked into this more deeply, I worked through my family, and I noticed my sister was the same, and my mother was also guilt-motivated. When I broke it down, almost every female in my family was so guilt-driven that they unintentionally avoided a beautiful and epic life, simply because they were too busy dealing with guilt.

When I was able to take a step back and say, "Wow, I actually *learned* how to be guilty for no reason," I was able to begin distancing myself from it. I was able to see how worthless that acquired and learned trait was and began to *live consciously* enough to see each time it came up and begin to rewire my responses from guilt stimuli to something that served me.

Looking back, I wouldn't have left the really dark and manipulative situations I put myself in if I had allowed that programmed guilt to stay in me. Think of the butterfly effect: even one small belief changes the entire course of life.

So, this idea of knowing what is you and what is not you is to better understand your programming. What have you unintentionally picked up along the way in life, from childhood and beyond, that no longer serves you? What preregistered responses do you have for things in life that really aren't the best reactions? When someone shows you they really love you, are you programmed to shut down and not receive that love, or to do something to slowly mess it up subconsciously? *That's your programming.* That's something you learned from someone else when you were a moldable little human being and perceived the world a certain way based on an experience or thread of experiences, and you built a perception around it.

Most often, these programmed ways of believing, reacting, and living are not serving you. *At all.* They are actually robbing you of the chance at a beautiful life. You may have picked up some beliefs that aren't yours in life; it's time to figure out what they are and set them down. Now, every once and awhile you may have programming you want to keep. That's awesome too! I grew up around strong, loving, independent females my whole life. I saw how it didn't serve them, and how it did. It helped me chase my dreams fearlessly, to take care of myself financially all these years, and to never think that men and women were capable of any different levels of success.

My objective for this chapter is to help point out your self-defeating belief systems that you may have inherited from various people so you can finally deny them access to yourself.

You won't be able to attain authenticity if you continue to live in the belief systems that other people have imposed on you. By stripping yourself of these detrimental belief systems, you free yourself from the burden of self-conflict, unhappiness, and frustration. It's extremely difficult to become what you want to be in life when you are shackled by the drama and beliefs of other people.

Take this example that happened to me. A friend approached me and said, "Hey, you are very qualified in what you are doing. Why not let people know about your college degrees and other qualifications so you can promote yourself more with people?" After she had said this to me, I paused for a bit and reflected. *Was she telling that to me?,* I thought. Or, was she mirroring herself in that conversation? I approached her and said, with love, "Did you mean to tell me something about my worthiness, or was that actually an issue that's bothering you?"

She confided that the "being more qualified" was her issue, not mine and that her statement was a mirror of herself. My friend admitted that she had been feeling less than adequate for someone she was in a relationship with. She found a way to release her unworthy feeling to me through that conversation and even live consciously in that moment. Her belief system, in a nutshell, was: You are not good enough until you prove it. And guess who gave that belief to her? Her environment growing up and her work situation for the past twenty-five years.

If I wasn't grounded or conscious, I could have easily grabbed the belief system she was passing to me. The suggestion that I should have to show my worthiness to other people first before I attempt something could erode my confidence, and because I highly respected her, I could have taken her advice, thus losing my authentic belief. Everyday, people we encounter send out unfiltered belief systems in many "innocent" ways. If we are not careful, we could absorb these belief systems and adopt them as our own.

After my "aha" moment, I approached my mother and asked her about the different beliefs and mental models that she has passed on to me. She told me that she had inherited them from her mother and passed them on to me. Imagine: I've been living someone else's belief systems for most of my life. No wonder I had so much unhappiness in my past—because those beliefs didn't serve me well. Those were meant for my grandmother. What works for my grandmother or my mother won't automatically work for me. Maybe it didn't even work for them!

Creating a Belief Inventory

As a technique and exercise, try this:

- Get a pen and a paper and write your current belief systems in multiple areas such as love, relationships, career, money, sex, religion/spirituality.

- After jotting down your belief systems, ask yourself: *Where did I get this?*

- Then, probe deeper: *Is this still serving me well? Is this making me happy? Unhappy?*

- If not, ask again: *What's another more serving belief that I could replace this with?*

Now, start living in that version as often as possible until it is made routine. Rewiring old beliefs can happen instantaneously when you find your truest thoughts, but it will require that you live consciously to be aware of when your subconscious takes over and uses a stored response to something instead of an authentic one.

Closing Reflections

When we were children, we had no control over the beliefs that influenced us, especially if they were coming from our parents and people of authority. It's important I tell you that you do not need to feel guilty if you are throwing out the beliefs that your parents, teachers, or past mentors have given you. This is not about them being wrong or right. This is not a moral choice. You simply want to find the beliefs that still serve you well and those that do not.

Prayer to the Universe

While I bask beneath the gentle enlightening light, grant me the wisdom to see the belief systems that cause me unhappiness, misery, frustration and guilt. Inspire me with inner strength so that I can detach myself from these self-defeating beliefs. May my authentic self shine like one of your glorious stars in the cosmos.

Chapter 3: Grounding

When I first set out to help others find the happiness I had found, I realized that there was going to be a mix of mental, physical, and spiritual shifts necessary to really make concrete life changes. I want to gift you with a grounding technique I use almost every day. Grounding is the process of connecting with our inner self. This is achieved by conscious breathing and silent meditation. Most schools of spirituality—if not all—teach the importance of conscious breathing. Learning how to breath correctly is one of Yoga's fundamental precepts. In Eastern meditation, breathing helps in harmonizing our spiritual faculties. By breathing consciously, we allow the breath of life to cleanse both our lungs and our thoughts. Breath is the purest manifestation of life. Once breathing stops, everything stops, so remember you have massive potential when you understand fully that if you can control your life force, you can control everything else you experience.

Whenever we ground ourselves, we root our being (literally, like a tree) to our deepest core through conscious breathing and silence. It's like swaying around throughout the day but not being uprooted and carried away into dramas. Even if you don't meditate, this is a huge help as it is an interactive visualization process you can learn. I would suggest doing this every morning when you wake up. We think we wake up fresh every day, but in reality, your energetic field is most susceptible at night. Your subconscious is processing tons of thoughts, and if you sleep with a partner, your energetic fields are colliding all night. I would suggest grounding each morning to really get back to *your* energy and also to protect it for the day ahead while washing away any old energies that will not serve you fully.

Benefits of Grounding

Heightened gratefulness. Since we are connected with ourselves and the spiritual world, we become more aware of the beauty and wonder that surround us. We start to appreciate the littlest of life's blessings. Our higher faculties become more sensitive to essentials.

Peace. By grounding our being, the daily hustle and bustle lose power to make us anxious and worried. We see circumstances for what they are, not for what we think they are.

Grounding Techniques

- Sit or lie in a quiet place where no one can disturb you.
- Turn off any gadgets that may distract you and try not to let the kiddos disturb you.
- Close your eyes.
- Take deep breaths.
- Breathe in and pause three seconds before breathing out.
- Guide your body to relaxation.
- Imagine your spine, your center, connecting to the earth.
- A tree trunk comes out from the base of your spine.
- Now imagine roots coming out of the soles of your feet.
- These roots go deep into the ground, to the center of the earth even, pulling you close.

- Feel the connection between you and the ground.

- Then, imagine a bright golden light touching the top of your head.

- The soothing light starts to trickle down from your head to your body.

- Picture yourself inundated by this light, you're glowing.

- Bask in this scenario as you continue to breathe deeply.

- Before waking from this state of being, be aware of your body.

- Slowly countdown from ten.

- Open your eyes and enjoy the new world that lay before you.

If you aren't used to visualizations, I urge you to give this an honest try over the course of our 30 days together. Come to it with an open mind and let it occur however you feel it needs to as you use this technique. I know you can do it :)

Prayer to the Universe

May every breath give me the peace that I am long

ground myself, bring me closer to my authentic self. Manifest the love,

peace, and happiness that has long been buried inside of me. Draw

them out so that I can allow my light to shine and share this peace with

the world.

Chapter 4: Self-Forgiveness

I remember a long time ago I sat and considered all of the things I was most shameful for. The people I had hurt, both unintentionally and intentionally, and realized as much as I had forgiven myself I still had a few remnants that needed to be worked on. Most likely, you have done something, or not done something, to someone or to yourself that needs healing, and usually, the hardest person to forgive is yourself. We can forgive other people and even offer excuses for the wrongs they have done to us. But why is it that we are withholding that compassion from ourselves? We deserve to be forgiven just as other people do—perhaps not because we justify the action, but because in order to grow and leave behind the old part of us we are shameful for, we must be able to truly release it through forgiveness.

In all the individuals I have worked with, and what I saw within myself, is the idea that our inability to forgive ourselves is rooted in self-unworthiness. This unworthiness comes from several inner issues. People in our lives might have influenced us to impose standards that do not serve us. Experiences might have compelled us to place ourselves in a box and define our fulfillment with checklists and crazy rules. We think that our lives are one big mistake because we have not lived according to the expectations of others or the rules we placed on ourselves for fulfillment. For this, we beat ourselves up out of guilt and refuse to forgive ourselves.

Now, the possible, and harsh reality is that you might actually find a secret comfort in "being down." Self-pity has a way of seducing in ways we are not aware of. Hate to call it like it is, but, you love your drama. You're unconsciously addicted to it. The reels you have playing in your head, they make you feel safe. Even if they bring you massive pain, at least you can count on knowing how you will feel. I remember talking about this with my partner just a few weeks ago. Imagine you're in an empty white room with two doors in front of you. One door is open; you can see inside. The other is closed, and you have no idea what's behind it. It's hard to choose the closed door simply because we have no ability to predict what it will be like inside. Our human brain starts searching for a rope to hang onto, but the closed door doesn't have one. So even if the rope is fraying in the open door, we at least have a sense of certainty that the rope exists. Get really honest with yourself: humans don't do things that don't have a reward, but sometimes our perception of rewards are so twisted, we can't see that everything that is recurring unpleasantly in our lives is actually giving us something in return; at least that's our screwed up perception. So, it could actually be that by not forgiving yourself, you are subconsciously receiving a reward for it. If you fall into this category, it's time to figure out what the reward might be.

Humans have basic needs, and I believe one of them is the need for certainty. The need to know what to expect. That's why a lot of new entrepreneurs' wives or husbands go nuts when the business is failing. It is not meeting their level of certainty that bills will be paid and mouths will be fed. Now, that may seem like a fair need, but are you differentiating what your needs for certainty are? How deeply they run and how much they may be sabotaging your truest form of you? I guarantee the higher level of you is far more courageous than the certainty-driven you. Let's find a healthier balance of the two, yeah?

Without self-forgiveness, we lose our other powers—to love, to create, to emphasize, to inspire, to motivate. It's really difficult to have enough energy to provide light when you're enclosed in a self-made dungeon.

However, when we forgive ourselves, we are able to embrace our vulnerabilities without negative energy surrounding the situations that brought forth the feeling or need for forgiveness. Admitting that we have committed a mistake—no matter how huge—is the first step to personal accountability. By acknowledging our mistakes or shortcomings, we create a larger inner space for growth and learning.

We free ourselves from the false deceptions of our ego. No human being is perfect or without flaw. I mean, how boring would that be? Instead, let it be part of your dance and raise to a higher level by owning the flaws and weaknesses and resolving to transform them into opportunities for growth.

We become more forgiving and accepting of other people. The root of social hate is self-hate. Self-hate springs from our inability to forgive and accept who we are. Sometimes, we hate other people just because they reflect the flaws we see in ourselves.

We are able to create lasting and meaningful friendships with ourselves and others. The key to having good relationships with other people is having a good relationship with ourselves. For how can you love others to the fullest if you don't love yourself first?

Techniques

- Look back and write all the "mistakes" that you have made in your life.

- Identify which mistakes still bother you. Ask yourself why.

- Is that reason rooted in someone else's beliefs about that type of mistake?

- What lessons have you learned from this mistake?

- What are the consequential burdens that you are carrying because of your inability to move on?

- Go through the grounding process.

- Forgive yourself—verbalize it: I forgive myself for these mistakes. Find a way to be grateful for them.

- Let go of the dark emotion that has been bothering you.

Closing Reflections

Holding on to your guilt has absolutely no value in your life. Your inability to forgive yourself only piles up into useless long-standing burdens that drag you down. If someone were to ask you to carry a sack of rocks on your back for one hour for no reason at all, would you carry it? No way! Yet that is exactly what you do when you refuse to forgive yourself. You carry a sack of rocks when you refuse to let go of your guilt. You use and waste so much energy, time, and emotion over nothing! All you have to do is drop it, walk away, and move towards higher goals and purpose. Say no to self-pity-inspired drama.

Prayer to the Universe

With love's nurturing and gentle presence, I look back on my life and see the mistakes that I have made. I see the faces of the people that I have hurt, the chances for betterment that I've squandered, the blunders that I feel may have cost me.

I choose to realize that guilt is like a chain that I lock around my limbs, a burden that I carry on my back and a dungeon of self-imprisonment. I free myself from the madness of creating my own unhappiness by emotional self-flagellation.

I now pile all the dark mistakes like a pyre. Sending light to burn them until they are ashes—until they are no more.

Chapter 5: Processing Energy

So it has become more widely understood and accepted that everything is energy, right? We hear about it often, but do we really get the depth of a statement as powerful as that? If every freaking thing is energy, we don't understand much at all, or our lives would usually look drastically different.

There is an entire science to it, but you'll have to check out my Authentic Manifestation program to dig more into those particular concepts, so let's focus on being able to process it on an emotional level. Now, we release those energies through our emotions, thoughts, and actions. In the same manner, we are capable of absorbing the energy that radiates from other people. Just like natural elements, there are energies that we should process before giving them out to the world or before absorbing them from other people. Becoming aware of your inner energies and emotions and how to process them can serve your higher self massively.

There is an ancient Eastern saying that goes, "You cannot prevent a bird from flying over your head, but you can prevent a bird from building a nest over your head." So, we cannot prevent emotions and energy from going through our inner system, but we have the ability to choose which emotions are allowed to stay and build a nest. Thus, to process emotions is absolutely necessary in our quest for authenticity.

Unprocessed emotions carry toxic heavy energies that make our minds foggy and disrupts the stability of our emotions. You know that feeling when you get into a fight with a loved one, and you just feel drained after? Or mentally foggy? There's a buildup of energy that needs to be removed. You can call it processing your thoughts, or your emotions just ran too high, but basically, there was a massive amount of disharmonious frequencies bouncing around, and you were affected.

Real quick, I need to give you this gentle reminder: It is *not* normal to feel like crap after talking to people, doing certain things, or having certain thoughts. We've just gotten so used to being bombarded with energy and not processing it that our threshold is assumed to be *way* higher than it actually is. If you leave energy in you that needs to flow through, you can literally get sick or manifest a heap of other issues that will seem to show up out of bad luck. If you are carried by mood swings and let raw emotions dictate the vibes of your day, stop and ask yourself, "Do I feel in control right now?"

How to Process Emotion

Contrary to what you may be thinking, processing emotions is a fun and rejuvenating activity. Even negative emotions can be transformed into positive ones. You have got to get a handle on how you process negative energy and even what you perceive as negative energy! Once you bring it to your consciousness, you'll be able to know how to change it, transmute it, or remove it completely. When you are pent up with emotions, do some physical exercise or activity. Take a walk, run, cook, dance, go to the outdoors—sweat it out. Get to your journal and jot down what you are feeling and the circumstance that created those emotions. Awareness is a key component here.

We shouldn't be afraid to feel our range of emotions whether they are perceived as negative or positive. We embrace and acknowledge them as soon as they come. "I am really mad right now. I am so sad and disappointed." Remember? You cannot prevent the bird (your emotions) from flying over your head, but you can prevent those emotions from nesting in your heart. So as soon as you feel and acknowledge them, ground yourself until the emotion settles down. Clear your mind and start doing a physical activity.

As your heart mellows, your mind becomes clearer, and you will be able to think straight on the best way to handle that circumstance that caused the emotion.

Closing Reflections

Imagine that deep inside yourself you have a conveyor belt. There are different kinds of bags and packages on that conveyor belt representing your emotions. Although all of them are your bags, you have the ability to watch them with detachment and decide which ones you should pick and bring back home.

Prayer to the Universe

I am grateful for my power to feel and radiate emotions. It means that I am alive and receptive to the prodding of my being and that I have the ability to feel. I embrace my emotions, even those that are sad, disappointing, and frustrating. For, by embracing them, I take control and grant myself the chance to transmute them in a way that can best serve my purpose.

Chapter 6: Perceived Rewards

Human beings are a reward-driven species. Yet, we have this extra "ability." We have the capacity to find rewards in negative issues and circumstances as well. Being that this is possible, we have to look at what types of rewards we are really after: real rewards or perceived rewards. Real rewards help us become authentic, while the perceived rewards rob us of our desired life experience.

Untangling Programs and Patterns

So, let's take a look here. At some point in this book, you may create some resistance to either the lesson of the day or what it brought up for you. You might even get a little frustrated at me. When we keep hammering patterns and programs that you have become so accustomed to, and that have even become a part of your identity, you can become a bit defensive sometimes. These programmed belief systems or patterns of behavior are parasitic, and they don't usually go down without a fight. And let me make this clear: I still have patterns and programming show up sometimes. It doesn't run my life anymore, but sometimes some seriously deep-rooted stuff comes up. Just a few days ago, I was in this super funk, and this huge wave of "I haven't been doing enough of my purpose work" was coming up. I asked a trusted friend for help with it and actually found myself getting defensive and trying to prove him wrong as if he were accusing me of something bad. It took me about five minutes (I live consciously now, so I rewire quickly) to realize he had an important message to give me from the Universe and I was rejecting it right after I had asked for it. The conversation ended really well, and I learned the lesson I needed to, thus catapulting me further into self-love and acceptance, which dominoed into my purpose work after all.

So allow this chapter to humble you, and find a deep honesty in yourself so that you can uncover what possible perceived rewards are running your show. You're not alone. Together we can crack open that hard shell that keeps your authentic self from shining through.

Perceived Rewards

When we engage with people—our partners, parents, coworkers, friends and even enemies—we are reward driven. It can be subtle, and utterly unconscious, but it's happening. For example, I had a client who seemed to lead a double life. He was a strong and very successful entrepreneur by day, and then became very closed off and quiet when he spoke to his mother. This quiet behavior would always lead his mother to comfort and question him. All the while, he acts as if nothing is wrong, but his behavior clearly causes her concern.

What I made clear to him was that he had a perceived reward for acting as he did towards his mother—he believed if he was closed off, he would receive the most energy and attention from her. Now, that may not seem like a problem, and he certainly wasn't doing it consciously, but two negative points were coming from this.

1. He could not directly connect emotionally with his mother because this method made him feel "safer" about love.

2. He was causing his mother unnecessary distress. He wasn't really upset, and she felt as if she failed as a mother because of it.

Not so authentic, eh? Nor was it bringing anyone happiness and peace.

Humans don't naturally do things that cause them pain. We do things because our tainted perception tells us it will be rewarding.

For example, if there is a large, or even small, part of you that doesn't believe love is a safe thing, or that relationships are actually not a good thing to experience, you'll avoid relationships, and even the reward of being alone or in an unfulfilling relationship is still greater than a healthy and fully loving one, because you may lose what you really wanted. Best not to have it at all, right?

In that example, allowing yourself to be open and vulnerable is not a perceived reward. But, is it equating to happiness? If not, we simply need to understand and shift the perception of the rewards we allow in our life. In your old self or programmed self, you created these perceived rewards to keep safe.

Your most authentic self can be free—loving freely, experiencing life freely, giving freely, whatever it is. By first consciously understanding the belief, laughing at how silly it really is, we can start fraying the thread of attachment to the false idea of safety and bring in a new and more serving belief.

Surviving Versus Thriving

I used to take refuge in emotionally unavailable friends and relationships, to the point that I would sabotage some of them if it felt like an emotionally vulnerable experience. Now, I am experiencing life on a much grander scale. We are here not just to survive. We are here to thrive. If you are operating from an old paradigm of your perceived rewards, then you will never reach your authentic self. You become a victim of programming. I'm here to show you that if that happens in your life, it is by choice. It may have been an unconscious one, but the tools I have given you in this book will surely make them conscious now. You know that saying, "Once you open your eyes, you can't close them again"? That's what I'm doing for you.

So, you react to current life situations according to the trauma when you were a child or the pain from your past relationships. This is meant to protect you. This makes total sense. You did it out of love to protect yourself.

Now you have different ideas of your perceived rewards, but the behavior pattern has likely solidified itself in your subconscious. Cool, then it makes logical sense that if it got there by circumstance, we could remove it too.

When someone tells you a truth about yourself, sometimes you just feel bad or shameful. Worse, you go into self-pity—but if you do that, then you likely see self-pity as your reward. In reality, though, it's an opportunity for growth. Consider it constructive criticism and remember you're allowed to tell someone that if they are going to help you with this, that you need them to deliver the information in a way you can receive it without shutting down. I always ask that when I am receiving information that the individual gives the message with love and encouragement, so my subconscious perceives as it a good thing and not something to block. It allows me to implement the necessary changes that much faster.

Now, it would be wise that when you experience that perceived reward, such as self-pity, you have to remove the veil and ask, "What am I getting from this reaction? What am I getting from this decision in my life? Why do I continue to stay in the shitty job that I don't like? Why am I in a relationship that I don't want? *What* is my perceived reward?"

Your answers to these questions—and similar questions—determine whether you are content with just surviving or ready to move towards thriving.

Examining Your Reward

If you find yourself externally or internally complaining about your circumstances in life, yet you are not doing something about them, you have perceived or subconscious rewards that are meeting some outdated type of need. Something you are thinking is benefiting you.

Whatever it is that makes you tolerate pain becomes an excuse not to reach your full potential. You must change your perception of your reward.

- What are you getting from the way you think?

- What are you getting from feeling the way you feel?

- What areas in my life, or where, did I possibly pick that up?

- How did I believe that it was the safest or smartest way to operate moving forward?

- What would a more conscious and healthy way to deal with these experiences be, moving forward, that I can commit to?

Prayer to the Universe

Awaken me from the foolishness of going after false rewards. They are traps that keep me from my authentic self. There is absolutely zero value in the rewards I get from my victim self. Make me see the real and truest reward is the attainment of my authentic self if only I let go of my attachment to my self-defeating mindsets.

Chapter 7: When Life Throws A Curveball

You can either empower or disempower yourself when "bad"
things happen. The whole concept of living an Authentic Life is so that
curve balls simply don't occur as often because being in alignment with
yourself has this funny way of protecting you. Alignment is another
word for intuition, and it's crucial that we see that following our true
intuition is like running in the woods barefoot and never cutting your
feet or stubbing your toes. The body is in rhythm with its surroundings
and naturally, avoids unnecessary hazards. Secondly, when curve balls
do show up, we can realign, quickly shutting down the amount of time
we use to "bounce back," and we can keep vibing on in our truth. Our
reactions are a choice, and when we see the beauty in our
circumstances, we can come to it without emotional charge, thus
keeping us in alignment. Knowing how to empower yourself when
unfavorable circumstances bog you down will help you stay on track

and push through life's trials with ease.

I remember a time when someone broke into a rental car I had and stole a lot of valuables. It was an unexpected experience, and I felt the initial surge of negative emotions while experiencing the harms done to me. Although the proverbial saying "don't cry over spilled milk" could be applied here I, as an authentic being, could go a step higher than that.

I asked two questions while my emotions swirled inside of me, the first being, should I choose to empower or disempower myself?

Had I chosen to disempower myself, I would have lashed out with bad energy and stayed stuck in a justifiable emotion for a while. I'd put a face on that criminal and imagine myself inflicting some sort of harm as my revenge. Then, all day I'd bring that emotion with me and allow that mood to affect everything that I did, thus changing my reality for that day. Imagine if I carried anger in my heart or head for a week and, due to that energy, I was not seen for my gifts I could give the world, or I wasn't able to help someone in need because I was so focused on my low energy. How many missed opportunities do we actually have in life due to being out of our authenticity?!

But I chose to empower myself.

After grounding myself, I accepted the fact that there was nothing more I could do to regain what I had lost. Second, I reflected on what lesson I could learn to benefit from this setback. Third, I rechanneled my thoughts on what I still had. Stacked against what I still had, what I had lost was nothing compared to the things I still possessed. I even decided to be grateful that they would benefit greatly from what they had taken, and I hope it fed the mouth of someone hungry!

We lose far more if we allow our distraught energy to affect our creativity and productivity. It's a massive waste to give too much energy and attention to something that is out of our control.

In that circumstance, it did not take long before I regained my inner peace and had a laugh. After acknowledging my emotion, I let it go by transmuting it. *But what is transmuting?* They say that there's a silver lining around each dark cloud. When we transmute, we create more silver linings until they are bigger than the dark cloud itself.

When life throws a curve ball, catch it and throw it back with a happy heart.

Prayer to the Universe

While I welcome abundance, love, and peace, I am not afraid to encounter distressing negative emotions. I will not cringe when they come nor will I allow them to scare me. I am capable of handling whatever life may throw at me, for I am empowered, bigger than any unexpected problems that may arise.

Chapter 8: Forgiveness

Ah, forgiveness. This is always a fun one, mainly because most people are dramatically on one side of the line when it comes to this concept. Someone either forgives someone when they "shouldn't," and they bury the pain, or they have no ability to let something go and carry the anger with them indefinitely. Both are so detrimental to the spirit, so it's best to get more neutral.

We relive the pain of the past whenever we remember the people who have hurt us, right? Our wounds open up again as soon as we revisit the wrongs that were done to us as if they were never given a chance to actually close up. Yet by pouring love on those hurts and channeling forgiveness, we free ourselves from that pain.

I had a client who committed what he perceived to be grave mistakes in his life, and he was massively shameful of them. He, too, had been hurt by people in his past. Lost and distraught, he couldn't break his pattern of guilt, resentment, and anger. He had been to over eight years of therapy, and he still could not disconnect from the past. He needed to forgive just as much he needed to be forgiven.

During my processing, I helped him arise from his low frequencies—negativity, fear, guilt—and step to his higher frequency. In that moment, he was able to confront his guilt and the anger he kept for the people in his past. Then, I guided him through the process of releasing his feelings to the Universe. He disconnected from the past and attained a higher frequency until he finally freed himself from his hurts.

Love & Forgiveness

Forgiving someone is difficult. Why is this so? Hurts inflicted on the heart are more painful than those inflicted on the body. When this hurt occurs, our belief systems play tricks on us. Our victim self steps in and fans our fire of self-pity. We sometimes see forgiveness as a form of weakness. Sometimes, forgiveness feels as though we are giving our power away.

As soon as we allow the victim in us to show up, it opens the doors to past hurts. It incites us to be angry at the people who have caused the hurt. When that unforgiving feeling starts to gnaw at us, we feel more resentment. Then the pattern of allowing the past to hurt us again and reliving the people who have hurt us replicates itself. We can disconnect from past hurts by "pouring love into them." Love. Love. Love. It is a quite vague concept, but as soon as you ground yourself, your heart finds a way to create love from pain—distill peace from distress and wisdom from confusion.

Prayer to the Universe

I hold in my hands all the people who need my forgiveness and all the people I need to ask forgiveness from. I now let go of all the past hurts and pain.

I grant them forgiveness just as I need to be forgiven.

After this, I unburden myself and step up to a new life filled with peace.

Chapter 9: Relationship With Food

We have a relationship with everything that is around us—people, our environment, and even with our food. Yes, *our food.* Everything is energy! Believe it or not, the relationship you hold with food, and everything that goes into your body plays a vital role in your entire well-being on an energetic level. Think of the varying emotions that we have around food. Our unhealthy choices of food affect our body and disrupt its functions. Food becomes a vehicle of toxins if not made in love to oneself. When we are no longer bothered by what we eat, it means that we have become numb to our bodies. If you can eat loads of sugar and not feel any side effects, it's not a positive! You have not reached a new level of enlightenment! It's that your body has now adapted to the crap you've given it. It no longer responds. Similarly to how an alcoholic can build up their tolerance and drink more and more over time, the body stops trying to process it and even reacts differently to it, thus manifesting liver, psychological, and cognitive problems at times. We start to spiral down when our body begins numbing the ability to communicate properly with us.

The topic of food is a touchy matter. Our relationship with food dates back to when were conceived in the womb. Food can either be a vehicle of nutrients or of toxins. Our food intake naturally affects all our bodily faculties. And, the state of the body is very relevant to the state of your being, our spirit. Thus, food actually has a direct effect to our authenticity.

This is the reason why there are ancient spiritualities that teach the regulation of food. There are foods that affect mood, quality of thinking, psychological disposition, and bodily functions.

If you're like the old me, you may have the tendency to overindulge in food during emotional highs and lows. Food easily becomes an escape outlet for unprocessed emotions. The appetite has a way of seducing our minds. It can convince us that an unhealthy "happy meal" could translate into a happy life.

I hit a very insecure stage when I was 18. Bulimia hit me first; I was way out of control of my emotions, so I'd eat to avoid them. I remember driving to Jack in the Box with strictly the intent to binge and then purge it. Makes me shudder thinking of how out of touch I was with my soul then. My bulimia turned into a bit of anorexia, I was 5'7" and just 97 pounds.

I grew out of all of those and chose to love myself, focused on healthy eating, ample calories, and loving my body fully.

In my own experience, I became lethargic each time I over-indulged. By overindulge, I mean I dishonored my body with processed crap foods, high sugar foods, or other toxic substances. My mind would get foggy. I'd feel a bit disconnected to the present moment. These are a few of the many ways our bodies can use to communicate, to tell us something. Food has the ability to generate emotions, but also, consider the emotion that may trigger the desired food in the first place.

This was my enlightenment: Food is just fuel. Nothing more.

When I started to view and treat food as mere fuel for the body, it cut most of my emotions with it.

When I was about to indulge in foods that my body did not appreciate, I would quietly ask myself: Why am I eating this? Am I doing this because I'm not dealing with an emotion? Am I making food a substitute companion because I am alone? Am I over-indulging because I need an outlet for my unexpressed sad or angry emotion?

By reaffirming the fundamental belief that food is just fuel, I easily get off the hook of unhealthy eating. It detaches me from food and views it as a vehicle of nourishment. With this attitude towards food, I make my choices based on that belief and choose only the food that can serve both my body and being.

Prayer to the Universe

I bless my food before I partake it, and with a pure intention, I eat only to fuel my body. May I learn how to detach myself from food so that I use it as a vehicle for nourishment. I will nourish my body because my body is my temple, the home of my spirit. Whatever I do with my body affects the state of my wholeness and my being.

Chapter 10: Choose To Learn The Lesson The First Time

Do you ever sit and wonder why some issues in life keep showing up? The circumstance and events that we don't want to happen become part of our life cycles. Why? In my opinion, these issues keep coming back for as long as we have not learned our lessons from them. There are times in my life where I literally sit and say out loud alone, "Okay, what am I missing here? God/Universe, hook it up yo, I need some help. What's the lesson I'm refusing to learn?"

You attract the same energy that you give out in the majority. If you want to remove the same old issues from appearing, it is time to choose to learn the lesson fast.

As a kid, I had this really great skill of learning through others. I remember watching friends make mistakes, or my older siblings get into trouble, and I would make sure not to repeat the behavior. That, however, didn't last, and on a subconscious level, I think I made a decision to start learning myself around age 17. You can guess how that turned out.

But as I sit here looking at my life and how I created my ideal human experience, I realize that I almost reverted back to my child-like self, but with a twist. I chose to learn lessons either *before* they occurred or, at least, the first go around. I didn't want to end up in relationship after relationship, job after job, or home after home not understanding why I had these patterns of behavior that were a disservice to my grand plan.

So, how do we stop cyclical issues from showing up?

The Cycle of Issues

Looking back in my past, I realize that my issues kept appearing in different ways or forms because I had not learned my lesson from them. The Universe will keep sending us back our issues as long as we have not learned how to grow from them. No new news here on the surface level, but if it's happening in your life, you're clearly not internalizing this concept fully. It's actually a beautiful built-in mechanism in the grand scheme of things.

Whenever we fail to learn a lesson, we retain the core negativity of that issue within us. We have not transmuted it. Thus, the issue settles inside like rotting fruit attracting flies.

There are people who go from one relationship to another with different people but who have the same core characters and attitudes. We wonder why some people finally end one abusive relationship only to find themselves in another. Why? Because they have not learned. Because that magnet of negativity is still intact internally.

In order for anything to change in our lives, we must first become aware. This means getting real with any negative anchors that have settled in your current programming and behavioral patterns. This allows for us to be conscious of what is really happening so that when we start getting hints that it is reoccurring in the future, we can actually avoid it without having to fully experience it. We already know where that road leads.

Living Consciously to Learn

You need not wait for weeks or years in order to learn your life lessons. Life is short, and the concept that "things take time" is crap. I personally watched some of the most influential people in my life stay in sick relationships that weren't serving anyone because they hadn't broken their patterns and begun learning the lessons they needed to. You can literally learn from a problem or an issue as soon as it pops up! Take them as learning experiences instead of trials, because you'll put yourself into a state of finding solutions instead of pain avoidance. By being conscious of your emotions and reactions to circumstances and situations, you can immediately process them. And don't worry, over time, grounding and transmuting your emotions will become second nature. You basically start creating this built-in force field that protects you.

Learn the lessons fast from the challenges and problems that come your way. Your authentic self will continue to emerge because there is nothing in you that hampers it from shining through when you choose not to hold on to the old patterns that were not serving you but that you were silently addicted to. Do not wait for years; the world needs you full force now.

Prayer to the Universe

May I learn from the challenging circumstances that are flowing to me. For every problem, there is a lesson waiting to be plucked. Make me realize that everything about the Universe is growth and expansion. I embrace the problems that I am running away from so that I can transform them into opportunities for growth.

Chapter 11: Releasing Expectations

I have this belief that life is a mixture of learning, growing, being, doing, and enjoying. Life immediately becomes difficult when you attach yourself to too many expectations. The reason I dislike having expectations (outside of business) is because it takes away your awareness of the moment—the happiness of the now. Sometimes, even if your expectation can come to fruition, you realize that you were not as happy as you thought you would be or you miss out on the beauty of the journey in getting there.

So, let's entertain a positive way to let go of our attachment to expectations.

Expectations per se are neither bad nor detrimental; I actually like them in certain aspects of my life. In many respects, creating expectations can be like having hope. It is a way of looking forward to something that we want to achieve or acquire. Desire is a stimulus for self-expansion.

However, expectations can start to harm you when you become overly attached to them—when you give them power. Once an expectation takes hold of you, it becomes the sole basis of your happiness and fulfillment, and that is when it becomes detrimental. You see a pin-sized drop of color instead of the masterpiece.

For the majority of my life, I was the queen of expectations; they ran my life. Now, it wasn't the expectations of my actions, such as I am going to make this amount of money this month or get into shape, that was detrimental. It was the expectation of emotional feeling that I expected things in life to give me. I had a very specific need I wanted things to fill, and when they didn't make me feel that way, I was in pain or constantly unhappy.

In a fuller understanding, it wasn't the actual outcomes that were so distressing. It was my attachment to wanting "things" or for others to fulfill an expectation I had labeled them with that robbed me of the actual joy of the process and what I could learn from it. It made me blind to the current blessings that I already possessed. I lived in an illusory future—a tomorrow with uncertain results that I tried to make certain so that I could feel safer.

So release your expectations by grounding yourself. Place those expectations in your hands. Appreciate the beautiful things and moments you want to create in your life. Then, let them go and free yourself from the burden or fear of not getting it. Do what you must to make your plan and your dream come true. Be committed to your plan of action completely. But leave your emotions out of it. After you have done all that is humanly possible, detach yourself from the results.

The beautiful irony is this: The results that we get are far better and bigger than what we initially expected once we detach ourselves from our expectations.

Prayer to the Universe

I cherish my dreams, aspirations, and plans. I imagine so much fulfillment as they come true. Yet, I know that if I cling to them, I turn my expectations into tools for anxiety and frustration. Now I realize that I lose the power to be happy in the now because my sight is obsessed with the future.

Chapter 12: Love-Based Decisions

Make every decision a love-based decision. When you are coming from the space of love, the decision becomes an easy process. Ask yourself before making a decision: Am I coming from love or from fear? Follow love and love will follow you. Now *love* is a beautiful word, but it doesn't resonate with everyone. Too "soft," right? So think of it this way if it's more fitting. When faced with a decision, which fork of that road makes you feel lighter? Which decision makes you feel heavier? Chances are, the one that makes you feel light, that comes from love, is the decision for you. It not only allows for you to do things you enjoy, but it keeps you in a calmer emotional state so that problem-solving and overall life outlook can come from a place of clarity versus frustration.

Typically the heavy decisions, or the fear-based decisions, come from a pre-programmed part of you—your logical mind, which has all of your stored responses and beliefs about life. What I see with this particular decision-making method is that it tends to include everyone else's beliefs, but not our own. Not the ones that will actually make us happy, or give us the life we so desire. Instead, it keeps us in a cycle of frustration and a false sense of safety. If you're anything like me, you can relate to a job or relationship where you made decisions out of fear instead of love. Even if it felt like the "right" thing to do, who was it right for? Who made you believe that those set of actions were the smart ones in the first place? *Where* did you receive those fear-based programmed beliefs?

To better appreciate and understand love-based decisions, let us look inside the anatomy of fear-based decisions. Look back in your life and count how many fear-based decisions that you have made. Think of the dire consequences that came from those fear-based decisions.

Here are examples of fear-based decisions:

- You are so afraid of scarcity that you decided to go into a venture without knowing your partners or the real nature of the enterprise. You were afraid that the offer was your last chance to become big. Fear moved you to jump blindly.

- You fear loneliness and being alone so much that you decided to go into a relationship without knowing the other person. You decide to remain in an abusive relationship because you fear no one else aside from your current partner will be able to love you.

- You are so insecure of other people that you decide to destroy them through gossip.

- You are so frustrated with your weakness that you decided that you cannot achieve your dream the right way. So, you resort to underhanded practices or avoid attempting to achieve them all together.

What do you think are the outcomes of these fear-based decisions? Remember that fear begets fear. Your fear-based decision will surely beget future monsters.

On the other hand, love-based decisions create love-based results. It carries no resentment, guilt, or frustration. You made your decision based on a pure intention. Since it is love-based, there is personal accountability. There is no else responsible for the result but you.

In my experience, love-based decisions are fruits of my intuition. After gathering all the factors to be considered before making a decision, I allow my heart to lead me.

Follow love and love will follow you!

Prayer to the Universe

May all my decisions be made out of love—nothing more, nothing less. Love protects me from frustration, blame, disappointment, and sadness. For even if my decision does not produce the results that I was married to, I know that I have not lost anything. I am aware of the bigger picture and that something far greater is in store.

Chapter 13: Your Higher Frequency

People living in a higher frequency are almost immune to negativity. Have you ever noticed that they just don't seem to get affected by lower vibrations from negative people? You can create that for yourself, and you will also elevate as a by-product. Choose to have a consistent awareness of the idea that you are able to live in your higher frequency, for this is the state where you best experience your authentic self and a beautiful life. Now it's important to consider first, are you at times that negative person? If not, why are you attracting negativity in your life? *No* guilt here; however, you must ask yourself *why* until you get clear as to the reason you are on a higher vibratory level yet allowing lower frequencies to bring you back down. Hint, the answer is likely in your pre-programmed rules about life.

What is Your Higher Frequency?

Let me give you an analogy for the higher frequency. This idea actually comes from a team member of mine, and it fits quite well.

Imagine that you live in a two-story house. You walk into the door and are on the ground floor.

When you walk in, there is a mirror, and you look through at the ground floor version of yourself. You see yourself, but you see a scary version. Your hair is thin, your face has no color, and your eyes have no spirit and sparkle. You, on that ground floor, see everything negatively. It complains unceasingly. All day, that self dwells in sadness or victim stories, not taking responsibility for life and having little positivity. This floor has so little sunlight, it's hard to see in there, and the air is thick and heavy.

Now, head towards the stairs and walk on up.

The second floor is the exact opposite of the ground floor. Go ahead, check yourself out in the mirror. This version of you radiates a happy and purposeful aura. Everything in that version of you is positive and pleasant. Your eyes look like your spirit could jump right out and dance around the room. Lastly, the entire floor is filled with light, and everything is arranged as you feel it should be.

The ground floor is your lower frequency while the second floor is your higher frequency.

We all carry those two floors inside of us. It is nothing to feel shameful of, but it does serve as an understanding that if both frequencies can reside in us, then we can choose to experience each as often or as little as we would like as well.

What Happens in the Lower Frequency?

When a distressing incident happens, your lower frequency response would likely go something like this:

Hey, freak out. Blame everyone but yourself. There's no getting out of this rut. So, just feel sorry for yourself—it's justified! Did someone hurt you? —maybe you should hurt back and vent out your anger. Are you in an abusive relationship? —Stay in it. You don't deserve someone better. Go ahead and start doubting and demeaning

yourself. Enclose yourself in this darkness and stop living. It's almost
impossible to get what you really want in life anyway.

Yuck, right? Yet, that is how we have been programmed or
shown to think at times, and we often use it! That kind of thought and
feeling generates vibrations. And, be warned—those vibrations are
everywhere. Negative people emit negative frequencies just like
everything else, and if you put yourself around it enough, it can
influence you and make you act and think like them. I remember
listening to Bob Proctor a while back, and he explained that when
you're on a high frequency, you are actually uncomfortable around
those vibrating on a lower or different level than you. What I take from
that is, if you keep yourself in a low vibrational environment long
enough, it may just pull you right down with it. When I set out to be an
entrepreneur, I had some seriously low frequencies attached to me.
Every time I tried to rise up, leave my job, leave my bad relationships,
it was as if those low frequencies had a cord attached to me and could
feel when the cord was getting tight as I rose up. Now, I don't think it

was ill-intentioned always, but those lower energies attempted to keep me with them, pull me back down. It wasn't until I said, "I must give my love to the world" that I created enough tension for the rope to finally snap.

Pay attention the next time you are near a negative person for a prolonged amount of time. Now pay attention to your behavior for a few hours after the encounter. What do your thoughts look like? How do you feel about circumstances? Any tightness in your body? This likely means you were shoved over into a frequency that is not your authentic self.

What Happens in the Higher Frequency?

Now bring that same issue or incident to our higher frequency. This is likely how the talk goes up there:

Hey now, ground yourself and clear your mind and heart. Pour love into yourself until you feel it permeate your whole being. Acknowledge those emotions and then let it go. Now, that you are at peace, affirm your self-beliefs— you are greater than any hardship, there is a solution to every problem, you are endowed with supernatural gifts to transcend anything that life throws at you. You deserve happiness. You can disagree with people without being disrespectful. There are no failures in life, for everything is a process. Make a love-based decision and rock a love-based reaction.

Same mind… totally different outlooks, totally different frequencies, and totally different realities as an outcome. Your higher frequency is the home of your authentic self. On that second floor, the vibrations are in harmony with love, peace, joy, and happiness. Everything is seen through the eyes of love and strength. No problem is too huge to need negativity. No issue is too complicated that it can't be solved.

How to Attune to your Higher Frequency?

Conscious living is a huge step in getting us attuned to our higher frequency. When we practice awareness, we stop living life from a reaction standpoint, but more so a proactive outlook. We know how we will handle situations from our higher self. The negative vibrations caused by people or incidents can't hit you because you've posted up shop on the second floor. It's almost like you don't even know what's happening on the first floor because you're so focused on the top. That is why it is important to stay grounded in order to remain rooted in your higher being.

Making periodic frequency checks can largely help in monitoring the state of our being. Figure out what those things are that make you genuinely happy. Meditations, exercise, journaling, singing, and recreation are my favorite ways to maintain the higher frequency of being.

Prayer to the Universe

I choose to experience a beautiful life while I dwell on my higher frequency. May I find no reason whatsoever to go down and wallow on that ground floor of negativity and squander the blessings and talents that I have been gifted with.

Chapter 14: Communicating Unselfishly

Communicating unselfishly means having the capacity to listen and speak with emotional intelligence. Humans have a deep need to be heard and understood. Gift that to others so you can also have that gifted onto you. By truly hearing others, you are able to gauge the channel and frequency of the person you speak with. It makes "mirroring" easier. By mirroring, I mean aligning yourself with the disposition of the other person so that when you want to be heard, you are speaking to them in the way they best receive information while still honoring yourself.

During discussion and conversation with a person, the ego has a way of taking over by instilling that intense desire to be heard, to cut off the other person. I was terrible with this with my honey, and he is so sweet he never brought it up. I actually caught myself doing it and had to ask him to not let me cut him off when he was speaking. He has massive value to give every time he opens his mouth, and I don't want to miss out on it because I can't control my own thoughts in that moment. Plus, it was just plain disrespectful of me. This kind of communication immediately creates a barrier between the people communicating and the energy that needs to flow to create an environment conducive to effective communication.

Mirroring

I learned mirroring when I was in sales, and in my experience, it's the quickest way to get on the same frequency. I allow the person to speak first and pour out his or her thoughts. The reason behind is not just common courtesy but because of my authentic self. Our higher being seeks nothing but the good of the person. In communication, the best way to gauge the frequency of the one we are speaking with is through mirroring.

While I listen to the other person, I immediately experience his or her vibrations, inner disposition, state of being and mental model. After gently observing all of these, I am now in the position to use the appropriate language, tone, content, and style of communication that would best fit the situation.

This way, I am able to adjust to the channel of the other person by getting on their frequency. Thus, my answers would be truthful and clear since I have adjusted to the other person's communication level and state of being.

Unselfish Communication

Being unselfish and less egotistical in communication is not just for a spiritual purpose. Think of communication as something like this: you and another are separated by a river, and each of you has to build half of the bridge to the other. If both of you start building at the same time, chances are your half bridges won't match. The trick is to allow the other person to build their half first so that it is easier for you to align your half with theirs.

This kind of communication is not always easy for people so you may be taking a bigger leap than others at times. Yet if we communicate with love, we are able to do this generously. By the time the other person has finished speaking, our authentic self has already processed the appropriate response.

Prayer to the Universe

I open my heart and my being to allow my love to emerge forth during my conversation and engagement with people. I leave my ego behind each time I speak to someone so that I can be silent and allow my higher being to understand with neither bias nor judgment. With a pure intention, I communicate with other people, knowing that my purpose is not to impose my intelligence but to create harmony, understanding, and enlightenment.

Chapter 15: Drama

All right, today is going to be a bit of tough love advice, so here we go. The majority of the areas of your life that are a mess are so because of your attachment to drama. There, I said it. The mental model of a victim takes an active function in the actual creation of a victim in multiple, if not all, areas of life. It becomes this reward system for someone's energy. People become easily attached to drama because they create it as their comfort zone. Drama and victim mentality become this inauthentic escape from responsibility. This can be happening on an extremely subconscious level, but if there is any area of your life you can't make sense of as to why it is the way it is… you may be addicted to the story or drama it is giving you on some level. It's time to let go of your drama and take responsibility for your decisions and actions.

You have got to learn how to become aware of, and then weed

out, any energy drama patterns so you can take full responsibility for your life. The reason is, if you're reading this book, you're not this far in and still unwilling to hear my words and feel the truth of the energy I pass on to you even in the exact seconds I am writing this. What that also means to me is you're willing to wake up and activate your gifts. You will not be able to give those gifts consistently or as powerfully if you are still operating in inauthentic and false realities. We have to pull back the curtains on all of our crap.

The Nature of Drama

So, *what is drama?* See if you identify yourself with any of these story lines:

- I struggle with love because my parents did not love me enough.

- I am a failure in my career because I am not skilled and talented, or I lack motivation.

- I am unhappy because I'm surrounded by negativity.

- I can't face my problems because they are just too

overwhelming.

- I'm not in a relationship because I get hurt, or I hurt others.

When you are in a victim mode (and yes, feeling shameful for victimizing others is still a form of victimhood), your mental model creates a sob story with you as the superstar. We create this slightly dark inner world where we can be free from some of the responsibility, and then we don't have to take accountability. The causes of your chronic unhappiness and misery are still perceived as being outside of you. It's easy to blame a broken childhood and a bad past relationship for our circumstances, but it's a disempowering, and honestly, it's an inauthentic way to live.

I remember a woman, whom I met years ago, who had a very abusive and troubling childhood. I don't say that lightly, but I will spare you the details. She, in turn, cheated on her loving husband, put her child in danger, and continued to blame the world that she was owed something. Her face was almost contorted with her chosen reality. Her husband put up with her hurtful actions and words, as well, because he felt she was a victim; he bought into the reality! Now, a few years later, I met a woman with an eerily similar and painful childhood. Although she was not married and still working through her pain some days, she ran a huge organization for children who needed help after abuse, and she was a smiling beautiful soul who lived a really wonderful life. Now, neither woman could erase the pain of their pasts, but look how differently they had handled it.

Consequences

Once you make drama your comfort zone, you allow yourself to sink deeper into that quicksand. Even if solutions and support are given, you sabotage your success and happiness because you have a current threshold of normalcy and anytime that ceiling gets hit, you bat yourself back down to comfort. It's okay to have a hard time admitting this, but fill this lesson with love and acknowledge if you may be exchanging your peace of mind and epic living for a few shekels of self-pity.

Letting Go of Drama

If somebody would give you a boxful of horse shit, would you accept it? What if it is wrapped up in expensive wrapping paper and ribbons. Why not? Because it holds zero value for you.

Choose to see that this belief system of drama is just exactly like that: a wonderfully wrapped box… of horse shit. If you see drama and victim mindsets like these, it is easier for you to let it go and resolve never to have them again. It might look rewarding, but it simply is not, and visualizations can be a powerful way to pull you into a more serving reality when you're clouded with false understanding.

Look at the areas of your life that aren't meeting your standards. *What isn't working?* Examine the belief systems that you have around those issues. Upon identifying the belief system, throw it away when it is no longer serving your well.

Be responsible for your actions and accountable for your decisions.

Prayer to the Universe

I choose to no longer hold on to things of lesser worth than my truest self. I have the greatest blessings of the Universe in front of me. I am throwing away the mental manure I am attached to and I am opening my arms to receive the natural flow of love, abundance, and peace.

Chapter 16: Nutrition

First, let me start by saying that I don't care if you ever get the six pack, or the toned ass. What I do care about is that you understand the power of a healthy body. Of a clean temple. Health problems are no joke, whether it's that you eat chemical shit storms for breakfast, you drink or use drugs too often, or you over supplement.

In this human experience, you are gifted with a body, and although society has taught us to glorify it in ways that literally don't mean shit, it is, in fact, a beautiful tool. You know that saying, "mind, body, spirit"? In order for you to stay in a balanced state, and achieve and maintain your authentic self, you've got to figure out what nutrition needs to look like for you. I'm not here to tell you what supplements to take, or to have a green juice every day, but instead, I want you to use your intuition.

Honor your body by taking good care of it. Pay attention to how your body feels whenever you eat unhealthy food or use drugs. Your body is there to serve your mind and spirit, but it will not be able to do that if you allow for it to be poisoned.

We've been programmed by society and media to have a strong emotional attachment to food and really all things external. Strictly speaking, food is just fuel for the body, nothing more. But society and media have programmed people to identify the unhealthiest food products with happiness. All of the media hype around food can be summed up in this line: eat us and be happy.

So, the effects of unhealthy or toxic processed food have been downplayed because they could make you happy. You sometimes buy food not because of the food, but because of the hopefully desired state you want to achieve, yet never do.

If you are happy, eat *more* food to be happier.

If you are sad… again, eat *more* food to become happy.

Yet it doesn't work that way. Either on a very conscious level, such as a stomach ache or brain fog, or a slower subconscious level such fatigue or mood swings. The mind gets foggy when the brain is overloaded with toxins. You can't think straight. Eventually, momentum and that passion to act on life seem to be so far away.

So, *how can we fix that?*

First, let's strengthen your resolve by accepting your body as a temple. It is sacred. Your body is the temple of your beautiful spirit. You will find it easier to serve the purpose of your authentic self if you take proper care of your body.

The foods we eat literally have vibrations, and since we can agree all things are energy in some forms, those frequencies can, in fact, influence our thoughts and disposition. Organic food, vegetables, and fruits have higher frequencies compared to processed meat and fatty foods. If you consume lower vibrational foods, *guess what?* Your dominant vibrational state can also suffer.

Prayer to the Universe

Bless my temple with your presence and inspire me to honor it by eating nutritiously. Detach my heart from any inordinate emotions with food so that I see it only as a fuel to give me energy. Make me realize that my unhealthy choices would soon overtake me and create obstacles towards my journey to find my authentic self.

Chapter 17: Changing Your Intention

I have this belief that the intentions you have and the actions you use need to be in alignment. If they are not aligned, it causes unhappiness and frustration, and it usually is hard to see how or why it caused negative emotions.

I have this saying that came to me one morning: "The action doesn't have to change. Just the intention." What this meant to me was, it's not about what you want, or the end result, it is the energy you put behind it that will decipher if it occurs or if any repercussions will come from it—the *why* you want it and *what* you want to do with it. Let's say you're at work for a firm of some sort. There is a nasty coworker who is rude and condescending to you for no reason. One day, you see their computer unlocked, and they left some private information that is against company policy open. You likely have only one action here—to tell the boss what you saw. However, you have a choice as to the energy you put behind it. One can be to keep the company safe and abide by company policy, and the other, to get revenge on the nasty coworker. Same action, same outcome for your coworker, but totally different intentions. One almost comes from light, and one from the dark, *you see?* Remember that everything has a vibration, and I imagine doing something in revenge is a lot lower than simply doing the right thing. All energy that comes from you is, in fact, a representation of you. This also helps with reducing any negative kickbacks from the Universe.

Let's work on this... Compartmentalize your life and decide what your current motivation for each aspect below is:

- Relationship
- Family life
- Career
- Overall life satisfaction
- (Feel free to throw in others, such as physical health)

Imagine the perfect version that you want to have in each area.

Now, look at your actions and beliefs. Let's take your career for example. If you have not yet achieved that ideal version in that compartment, ask yourself if your actions are aligned with your intention. Perhaps you don't even have a job yet, or you hate your current job. Why is this happening if your intention is having a job according to your greatest version? Something is running amuck, right? Your actions are not aligned with your intention. And what if you've already got the career you wanted, but you find yourself still unhappy? You got your actions and result right, but your intention was incorrect, or perhaps impure.

How is this?

First, examine your relationship with your intention. Perhaps you really want that job, but you are afraid of the consequence —disconnection with your family, friends writing you off, or other reasons. That's why you might be unconsciously sabotaging yourself not to get that job you wanted to have. Your intention must be coming from your authentic self, the result that could truly serve you well.

Prayer to the Universe

I look inside of myself and check my intentions and my actions.

May they be aligned so that I am not derailed from my purpose of

becoming authentic. Intention without action is futile, and action that

fails to satisfy my intention is nothing.

Chapter 18 : Scarcity

The belief system of scarcity is one of the most destructive mental models. Just made it really real for you, didn't I? Haha. For real, though, scarcity-based thoughts and feeling prevent us from experiencing happiness and fulfilling the aspirations of our authentic self. I remember a time I lived alone and loved living alone, but I was always worried about saving money, spending as little as possible—where I spent an entire week finding people to live with me instead of spending that week finding a way to make more money. I was programmed for scarcity mindset, and the truth is, most of the western world is, too.

Voices of Scarcity

Here are some of the voices of scarcity that we tend to subconsciously entertain:

- There's not enough success going around…

- There's not enough money in the world...

- There are not enough jobs available for me…

Now ask yourself…

What areas in your life operate in scarcity right now? In what areas in your life are you accepting scarcity? How are you projecting scarcity to other people? Where did *you* receive your scarcity mindsets?

There are serious consequences for living on that frequency; for example, if you have the all-too-common mindset that loving people fully is not safe, you won't give your love freely. When you withhold love from the world because you think you don't have love to give, the world withholds love from you. Scarcity prevents the world from seeing you as you truly are. It prevents the Universe from giving you what you want because your actions don't make sense with what you say or pray for. I'm pretty sure your most authentic self wants to love the world—and it also wants to receive love, but in order for that to happen, you'll need to start with changing the scarcity programming that is running the show.

Energy & Alignment

So we can agree now that if you are dishonoring yourself by not showing the world love, you are not being authentic. It's so much easier to create when you're in alignment with yourself. You can certainly do the "brunt force" method—I did for years—but there's always a burnout every few months and a lot of discomfort along the way. When you are in alignment, there's a certain type of energy that erases those feelings of scarcity. They cease to exist, almost like you jumped into a new reality where certain feelings just don't occur in *that* reality. So look at the areas of your life where you are choosing scarcity. Be honest with yourself.

My Hand in Your Wound

If there are times you are resisting my teachings, saying: I am starting not to believe in Mandy... She's talking a lot of BS... I don't know what she's saying, but it makes me uncomfortable... Understand what I am doing. I'm offering you a lot of things that are like a hand sticking into the wound and opening it up so we can clean it out.

But that's the beautiful process of stepping into who you truly are. From your wound, I will draw out your worthiness so that all scarcity models die off. Scarcity is a tricky program and pattern. It wants to attach to you regardless of your effort to eliminate it. But when you are freed from it, it opens up space to attract people. To attract events and circumstances that serve your purpose. Life lessons just show up. It is easier for you to choose that truth. Life is absolutely incredible when you become who you truly are. Unworthiness and scarcity have absolutely no place in your authentic self.

Prayer to the Universe

How can I even think of scarcity when everything in the world is a reflection of abundance and generosity? All it would take is a gentle tilt of the head to look up and contemplate the eternal stars and the infinite universe. There is nothing scarce in the world. I choose to pull out the roots connecting my feelings and beliefs in scarcity. From this moment on, I am no longer a slave of false scarcity—I will be the child of abundance.

Chapter 19: Meditation

Each day we encounter different kinds of stress, and typically from several sources. Work, relationships, unhealthy eating, and even environmental stress. Meditation is meant to change your overall frequency. It creates an energy around your auric field that deflects negativity. Thus, you are able to handle stress more effectively. It allows for you to sit in the quietness of all you truly are and bask in Universal truth. I like to think of it as basically bringing you closer in oneness with God. It's in those quiet moments that you allow yourself to stop swimming in all of the energy constantly moving around you, and begin to actually become aware of it, to create a harmony around it.

Forms of Meditation

I like to think there are many ways I can meditate. The most simple and well-known form is to sit with yourself, be alone in your energy and just breathe, allowing for a feeling of oneness to settle in. I have to say, this is not an easy task for some, and others seem to be the "sit and do nothing" masters. This type of meditation is important; it allows you to create a space where you can remove yourself from the energy you have been swimming in all day and then integrate it into the whole and completeness of all that *is*. You are simply existing in those moments. There have been times when I have sat in this feeling long enough, and I actually stop feeling emotions. Everything simply… *is*. It's quite indescribable, but perhaps you can relate. If not, well then I am excited for you to apply more meditative practices in your life and reap the benefits.

Now, you may prefer to take a more active meditative approach such cooking, exercising, walking outside, driving, or journaling. This is great, too, and they all serve great purposes, so honor what feels right to you. Since the purpose of meditation is to align our frequency with our higher self and create positive vibrations, any activity that accomplishes that can be your meditation.

Stress and Meditation

So, as we can guess, stress is caused by an inability to cope with certain aspects of our lives, ourselves, or our surroundings. It's also an indirect killer of our bodies, minds, and spirits. Over time, stress can literally cause parts of ourselves to shut down, leaving the mind to absorb the stress, or the body to begin to absorb the dense energy that stress can trap inside of us. Back in 2015, I was asked to test my therapy-based coaching techniques in a clinic in Norway. We would basically hook the client up to EEG-like machines and measure, via energy, what was going on with the brain, as well as assisting in rewiring it, while I would work through the client's issues. At times, the client would have a psychosomatic issue, meaning something that was going on in their brain, whether it be stress from an old trauma or current life issues, that would have manifested itself into a physical ailment. Over the course of a few hours of speaking with the individual, and with the assistance of the technology, I would be able to narrow down the exact stressor that had caused the physical issue to create itself. I could go on for days about this, but I'll save that for another book. My point is, stress, even on a subconscious level, can do massive damage to the body, the mind, and of course the spirit because they are interconnected. In this human experience, they all intertwine, so meditative practices allow space for those issues to dissipate or, at a minimum, rise to the surface to begin the processing work of removing them before they run, or ruin, your life.

Meditation pushes away our mental blocks and relaxes the body. It empties our thoughts and calms our hearts. With a more peaceful disposition, we start to see our causes of stress in a different light. It's literally lifting a fog and changing your state. By being in touch with your higher self, or God, or whatever word floats your boat, we are made more consciously aware of how best to approach our challenges and sources of stress. We are basically telling our minds, as well as the Universe, "I don't like the way I feel, and I'm willing to do something about it." The Universe tends to hook you up once it knows that's the case, so it's important you meditate with good intention and never be afraid to ask for help.

I hold the belief that if something can occur in this human experience, there is a way to undo what it has done if we choose. This goes both positively and negatively. Look for the answers from the best place of peace you can get yourself to; even get yourself to a bird's eye view during your meditations and look down upon yourself and give yourself the loving words of encouragement you need to hear at that moment. By meditating, you allow for your intuition to grow in strength, and during your meditation or right after is a beautiful time to ask yourself questions you need answers to. Just remember, don't waste your time asking questions that you're biased on getting a certain response of. Your intuition doesn't always make logical sense, so make sure you ask from a place of detachment from the answer.

Prayer to the Universe

Teach me to calm myself and find peace amidst my struggles.
Show me the way to find my heart while I voyage through my personal
storms. The stress and anxiety that I have at times could be dispelled

the very moment I choose to dispel it. There is absolutely nothing that my authentic self could not handle or hurdle. Let me regain my love, my peace, and my serenity in meditation.

Chapter 20: Protecting Yourself

Humans are like sponges. We are capable of absorbing all kinds of energy around us, whether positive or negative, every day. Consider how you can feel pain or sadness simply through transference from other people. It's important you take this chapter lightly, or more correctly, that you understand that I'm not advising you run around with your hand up to people like a weirdo (although the visual is funny), but it's important to learn how to protect yourself from negative emotions and vibrations from other people. Be conscious and pull yourself away from people and circumstance that threaten your peace.

How I Shielded Myself from Negativity

While I was waiting in line one day when I was living in Florida, an old lady initiated a conversation with me. At first, I entertained her with openness and love. I listened intently to the things that she shared with me. But after some time, her sharing turned out to be nothing but a series of victim stories and gossip. Without being rude, I cut myself from the conversation and walked away. You should have seen her face; she was so deep in the energy she was attempting to draw from me unconsciously that she looked like she had seen a ghost when I ended the conversation politely before she could finish.

Had I not been aware of her frequency, I could have absorbed her negative energy and took it home with me. "Negative" people can drain us and sap our positive energy if we allow them to. Was I being selfish when I turned away from the lady? No, I wasn't. I love my authentic self enough to shield it from anything that could threaten my peace. I don't want the Universe thinking I'm okay with those types of interactions. Besides, there was nothing good that could come from such a conversation. Had I entertained the lady, like the old people-pleaser version of myself, I would have just fanned the flames of negativity by affirming it and been out of alignment with my true thoughts.

Radar & Shield

Now, when I say negativity, that's really a broad word. What I mean is something that is out of your truest alignment or someone who is vibrating at a completely different, and possibly "lower," space from you. When it simply won't serve you to dip in your frequency just to level with someone, that is considered negative. However, they may have a whole group of friends who totally vibe with them when they gossip or delve in self-pity; you don't have to teach them a lesson if they can't hear it. Just honor yourself instead. You should never have to do, be, or say things out of alignment in order to fit in.

We can protect ourselves from negativity by turning on our inner radar. The radar will warn us about the nature of people and the state of their beings. It will help us gauge if we are simply the dump of their complaints and drama or if we can truly help. This, of course, doesn't mean that we will turn away every person who wants to pour out or confide, but be aware of whether they are asking for an ear or help, and only give as much as you know you have to give without sacrificing your energy in the process.

We can differentiate people by their intentions. Victims tend to want to dump without any intention to change their ways and mental models. They just want to pour the poison in hopes that someone gets infected by it too. The saying "misery loves company" couldn't be truer here.

The other group of individuals is those who express their negativity in order to seek help and find means on how they can change. These people should be accommodated and helped by all means and with the tools in this book. I think you can probably point them in the right direction without giving more than you have to offer to them.

By keeping a healthy radar of awareness to others' intentions, we begin to deflect the negative frequencies and vibes that try to hold us down. You may also learn that you are one of those people who drag others down! Hey, no shame here, it's a great thing to know, and I've done it before unknowingly too. However, as soon as you're aware of it, you can choose to shift it and become someone who raises others up instead—a person whose presence can immediately turn off the negative energy in a room, those living in their authentic self, for example.

Prayer to the Universe

I bask in your authentic energy with a grateful heart for giving me so much love, peace, and happiness. Yet I should protect these gifts so that they will not be taken away by a deluge of negativity that transpires at times. May I be generous to people and love them without sacrificing my own happiness and peace. May I speak my truth with honesty, integrity, and respect for humankind.

Chapter 21: Your Temple

So, let's add on from yesterday. I see so much importance in establishing a relationship with the body that I am devoting another session to it. You are your own temple. If your temple is not clean, you cannot ascend. However, we talked about food already in the last chapter, so let's dig into a different component of physical health. There is a direct relationship between our body and being since they affect each other. The symbiotic relationship between ourselves and the bodies determines the quality of our thinking, feeling, and actions.

When I was in high school, I had this short period of crippling anxiety. I mean, I dreaded going to school because I would usually begin thinking I couldn't breathe and I'd have to leave the classroom. It was like suddenly my mind wasn't communicating with my body in a loving way. A few years later, I began this intense study into all things energy as well as the mind, body, spirit relationship. I eventually found myself in Bergen doing research in the realm of psychosomatic related illnesses. If you don't already know, psychosomatic illnesses mean that something that stems from the mind has now been made to manifest in the body. I began working through this with clients, figuring out why their heart issues, skin problems, and faulty organs were, at times, being caused by an emotional trauma or factor. Exquisite, right? I won't go into all the details of how, but what I can say is that your body is built to serve you and act as a compass for what your spirit or your mind may be needing or trying to tell you.

So, I say this because wouldn't it be wise to catch the issues and fix them before they get to the physical level? What about before they even get to the emotional level? Okay, I'm getting off topic, but consider this. If I have a weight problem because I was molested as a child, and I want to be seen as undesirable so that I will never risk molestation again, does that feel like the best solution to my fear? What advice would *you* give me?

That's what this is about: creating the relationship with your mind and body so that you can begin to process and work through the past and even current issues without allowing them and their dark energies to get stuck in your temple and create problems that then *further* pull you from who you are. The first step? *Awareness.*

We may be filled with good intentions and plans, but if our bodies are not healthy enough, we cannot act on them. In like manner, we may have fit and healthy bodies, but our minds and hearts are clouded. Both body and being should be harmonized to achieve our authentic selves.

For this reason, regularly detoxifying our bodies is a good healthy practice. When we periodically flush out the toxic and unflushed wastes from our bodies, we relieve them from stress and free them from elements that prevent it from functioning well.

The body's inability to flush out our excesses and our toxins is the main cause of our health issues. The foods we eat are either vehicles of nutrients or of toxic elements. Thus, food affects our state of being and our capability to connect with our authentic selves. Again, if all things are energy, that means foods, minerals, and nutrients all are energy too, right? They have a certain vibration or frequency, as well then, correct? It makes sense that we should fuel our minds with harmonious thoughts and our bodies with harmonious fuel. When we use our bodies as a means to attain our authentic selves, the motivation becomes more meaningful. It is strong enough to transform an unhealthy lifestyle into a healthy one.

Prayer to the Universe

I embrace my body, my temple, with a happy and grateful heart. There is so much wonder in how the body functions. When I contemplate how my body functions, I am lost for words to describe this amazing machine. May I love my body as it should be loved—a temple where my being dwells. I abstain from anything that could destroy it and accepts those who can nourish it.

Chapter 22: Your Sacred Ground

I grew up with the belief that unless I was the best, I was a loser. I was a people pleaser and fell into controlling relationships easily. I may have seemed like I had a backbone, but I didn't. I was like a chameleon, being whatever anyone wanted me to be at that moment. That led to a whole lot of inauthentic living. Jobs, relationships, friendships, even conversations with myself didn't feel… right.

Some of us are overwhelmed by the need to be perfect, and the inner workings of perfection look different from person to person. What I would love for you to take from this is that the need to be perfect keeps us from being authentic. If you've ever taken one of my programs, you'll notice that in each video I'm dressed in laid-back clothes; sometimes I don't use my camera crew, sometimes I don't even do my hair or makeup! It's my way of saying, "I am most comfortable this way today, and that does not disable my ability to do my purpose work or be good enough for the world today." It's not a coincidence! The first step in becoming authentic is being vulnerable and showing up in the world free from our needs to look or be perceived certain ways out of significance. Cease to strive for perfection just to please people. Standing on sacred ground means accepting your vulnerable self and refusing to trade your authentic self for the "perfect person" you feel others want you to show up as. It's like a treadmill: you'll burn plenty of energy, but you're not going anywhere with it.

By learning how to embrace your vulnerability, you can then actually expand yourself.

My Sacred Ground

So what is my sacred ground? It's like this beautiful inner space where I am vulnerable. There is this negative or false perception that vulnerability means weakness, but that's not what I mean when I use that word. It is sacred because this is where the truth about myself resides.

People are sometimes afraid to be vulnerable, to show other people who they truly are. Fearing rejection, they put up smokescreens and masks to hide their real selves. But our perceived weaknesses are as sacred as our strengths. I had this huge breakthrough in my life when I was sitting with a very high-level business therapist. I was explaining how I felt unless every single one of my clients saw massive results—I felt unworthy of helping them. I had multiple rules as to what "success" looked like, in such a way that I wasn't honoring what success even looked like to my clients! He said to me, "The rules and need to have perfection in your work… is what is making your work imperfect." It hit me like a brick. If I were to attempt to follow these false rules, I would miss the mark completely. I had no weakness that wasn't allowing for me to massively impact people; it was what I perceived to be a weakness that was stopping me from even trying. And low and behold, I kid you not, that exact client I was thinking about, you know, the one I "hadn't helped enough," messaged me saying when he began working with me, he was going to end his life. So although he is still working on attracting the relationships and working on the health, I gifted him with something far better. I gifted him with *life*. How could I wait and be stuck in my perceived weaknesses to the point that I stopped helping save lives? I was right back on track after a shift in simply a perception. Back to my authenticity of showing up however I am.

When your authentic self has risen, you are not concerned anymore about being liked or not being liked, in being accepted or being rejected. Since you have embraced your vulnerability, rejection and non-acceptance of people have no importance anymore. What is so neat about this phenomenon is you don't experience very much tension when you're living in your truth. Your vibration just attracts truth right back to you, and it's usually quite pleasant.

No one can humiliate you because you have accepted the fact that no one is perfect, and frankly, it's not the purpose of life. There is no need to be insecure about people who you may perceive to be better than or less than you because you know your own gifts and are aware that each person has different gifts for different life purposes. We are all pieces of a puzzle, and if we were all corner pieces, this masterpiece would never be complete. It's all totally perfect.

Strive to turn your vulnerabilities into strengths, *see* that they are from a higher place. No need to do this to compete or put yourself higher than someone else. Choose to rise up simply because you are following the call of your higher self to attain the greatest version of you.

Prayer to the Universe

I am free from the burden of pleasing people, of wanting to be accepted, of desiring to be loved. I have stood my sacred ground. I am aware of my worth and power. I do not need people to confirm my talent and capability before I serve or strive for my life purpose. My sacred ground is my safe space, my fortress, and my garden where my authentic self reigns supreme.

Chapter 23: Rewarding Yourself

I remember when I first met my partner. He loved getting massages, and even manicures and pedicures. I was in awe that he was so good at taking care of himself. I had had maybe five massages in my entire life before I met him!

Then I saw that my self-love was different. I exercised and danced. I spent lots of time alone journaling my thoughts. I'd sit in salt baths with candles.

I urge you to stop right now and see what you do for self-love. Does it make you happy and feel like you are in fact showing yourself love? Maybe exercise feels like a necessity to you and not self-love, so make sure what you're using for self-love is actually working in the way you want it to. Think of different ways to reward yourself. By loving and honoring yourself, you bid the Universe to do the same for you. By loving yourself, you also enlarge your capacity to love others.

The Nature of a Reward

Granting rewards is an innate psychological instinct. Society has always found ways to reward those who excel. Perhaps that is the only time you reward yourself too—after you've "earned" it.

The notion of rewarding yourself can be really hard at times due to a lack of feeling worthy. We tend to have a feeling of unworthiness towards enjoyment or good things in life if we feel guilty for something we have done in the past or we were raised to never be "good enough." Yet we don't struggle nearly as much when rewarding other people.

Why is this so?

There are belief systems that program people about receiving rewards from themselves. The very idea of self-love is not valid, or it is a form of selfishness. But true self-love is not selfish at all. Self-love is the foundation of happiness and love, and you can only help others drink when your cup is continually running over first. You can be the healthy example for others. When I was in my early twenties, I had someone very close to me in a very toxic relationship and unable to leave. Guilt and the feeling of being needed were running so strongly that this individual couldn't leave when they should have, no matter what anyone said. I decided I would live a beautiful epic life and show myself copious amounts of self-love, simply because I wanted to, but it had a deep effect on this person. Seeing me live life as I desired and not as the world might think I "should" indirectly granted this person permission to do the same, and years later they told me I was the example and proof they needed. Needless to say, if you see this individual on the street now, there's a bright light in their eyes, a pep in their step, and a beautiful new partner by their side, and they have helped many people since finding their authenticity. Far more than the one they thought they had to sacrifice and lose their own self-love for.

So, in essence, self-love means that we refrain from doing things that could harm our self-worth and our well-being. We honor all of the components that allow for us to live authentically and in alignment to our own truths. No one needs to tell us how to do it; our intuition can guide us when we listen to the whispers of our soul.

Ways to Reward Yourself

We need not resort to expensive ways of rewarding ourselves—although we should be able to do so without guilt. Materially, you could purchase something, such as a watch or a house, if having that would serve you well. Abundance should be experienced, and felt, without guilt.

Yet, we can also reward ourselves by simply taking a nice, relaxing bath or by organizing a dinner with close friends. Do something that you don't normally do and embrace the happiness it gives you, breathe it in, and see it as an act of love towards yourself.

Prayer to the Universe

I deserve life's best rewards. I am worthy. I acknowledge my greatness. I grant myself the joy I want to experience by gifting myself with things or actions that can honor my authentic self.

Chapter 24: Authenticity

I mean, come on, you didn't think you were going to read a book about authenticity and not have a chapter about it, right? Let me borrow Marianne Williamson's most inspiring words:

"Our deepest fear is not that we are inadequate. Our deepest fear is that we are powerful beyond measure. It is our light, not our darkness that most frighten us. Your playing small does not serve the world. There is nothing enlightened about shrinking so that other people won't feel insecure around you."

Yes, yes, yes! See how often we are actually playing small? Like my experience with my business therapist, we believe perfection (however we may perceive it) is what will get us to the end goal. *False*! That is what has us running through a damn maze, getting our arms scratched and our toes stubbed. When you refuse to be authentic, you're actually settling for being mediocre. You play small. Why do you allow yourself to shrink? Okay, internal check in. Do you do any of

the following?

- Live your life according to expectations, choices, and

  dictations of others (this includes your closest family

  and friends).

- Sabotage yourself by withholding your talents because

  you are afraid of success or being "seen."

- Play small because you are afraid of making other

  people small or inferior.

- Settle in relationships that do not serve you well because

  you have "no other choice."

If you've said yes to even one, then you're playing small, and

that is in direct relation to being inauthentic. It is impossible for you to

stand in your authenticity and not feel like *more* than enough. Direct

alignment is a place of wicked awesome peace, and you tend to fill up

your soul and those around you just by being truthful to your

powerfulness.

Confronting Authenticity

I regularly have an "authenticity check" to make sure that my true self is not "playing small."

I confront my belief system and ask: Is this still serving me well?

I take hold of my activities and question: Does this makes me happy?

Before undertaking a venture, I inquire: Is this according to my purpose?

When I am not authentic, I also make other people suffer because I am unable to serve them at the highest level. I deprive them of the wonders that I can do when I operate in my highest self.

Prayer to the Universe

We were born to make manifest the glory of

God that is within us.

It's not just in some of us; it's in everyone.

And as we let our own light shine,

we unconsciously give other people

permission to do the same.

As we are liberated from our own fear,

our presence automatically liberates others.

Marianne Williamson

Chapter 25: Core Values

My core values are what I stand for—authenticity, love, expansion, integrity, servant leadership, and truth. But simply stating your core values means diddly squat if you're not actually living them. Examine yourself right now. Write down your core values and then look at your life. Are you living in alignment with those values? Not here to guilt you, but tough love is still love. Perhaps you're not living them because they aren't actually the values that will get you to your authentic self, to fulfillment. They just sound good on paper and make your ego feel good. I want to guide you on how to form your truest core values.

What Are Core Values?

Core values are the values that guide your life, your choices, and your actions.

Organizations, institutions, and companies introduce themselves by stating their vision, mission, and the values that help them achieve their purpose.

Likewise, as an individual, it would serve you well if you craft your own vision and core values. This would help you make authentic life choices during dilemmas and complicated life situations.

Claiming Your Core Values

How do you come up with your core values?

Look back in your life and see what were the values prominent during your most trying times.

Look at your current life and see what core values you need to acquire to serve your purpose or achieve what you desire.

What are the core values that are not working? Let them go and rewrite them.

What are the beliefs that you have inherited that don't serve you well? Maybe no sex before marriage was a great thought, but you already broke it and need to release the guilt of it all. Let them go and rewrite them.

After listing these core values, commit to practicing them in everyday life.

Practicing Your Belief

It is very important that you align your life with your core values. It is useless and empty to list your core values but not practice them when the situations for them arise, so don't have values that you don't actually care to live by; again, there's no room for judgment or ego here. Core values are wings that can make us soar above life's daily problems. They support the purpose of our authentic self.

Prayer to the Universe

I become authentic by living my core values, by practicing my beliefs in daily life. I allow myself to shine and become an inspiration to others through my words and actions. I shall treasure my values as if they are jewels.

Chapter 26: Why Not Have It All?

One of the most prominent and recurring belief systems that we have inherited from our childhood is the "and/or mentality." But this mentality prevents us from fulfilling our potential. You short-change yourself when you have to choose between two desired options, and this day and age, it's usually an unnecessary and outdated way of thinking. Start asking yourself: *Why can't I have both?* I had this belief that if I wanted to a lot of money, I had to work really hard. But then, if I work really hard, I will likely not have much time to enjoy life because I will spend my hours working. How will I be around for my future family? What if my children hate me because I will always be work focused? What will I miss out on? It's a constant cycle of what I want but can't have both of—so I was constantly torn. Not only that, but it was complete bullshit. My programming was running wild and deciding how to feel and what to think to keep me from chasing my dreams, but until I decided to envision a different reality where I could have it all, it wasn't happening.

Now, I know that I can still make money and at the same time enjoy my life; in fact, I have proven it. Since I achieved that belief, I have had the best years of my life. I accepted the truth that I can have both. As soon as I declared that belief and solidified it in my mind, both showed up—almost instantaneously. What I am teaching you is that you can be authentic and be fully loved and embraced for who you are... *you can have both*. But the first step starts with simply *believing* that you can have both. We don't have to live in the "I can have this or I can have that" mentality anymore; the Universe can be far more expansive and wonderful than that.

As creators of our own reality, if we don't want that to be our truth anymore, we just have to remove it from our choices. By asking ourselves bigger questions, we gain understanding on what serves us, and we can be strengthened to take radical action. How can I have it all? If somebody wants something and I want the complete opposite, instead of going "who should lose here," I ask, "How can we both win?" We may not have been raised to believe we can have it all, but now, as conscious adults, we can choose to see how having it all is actually a great, and real, possibility.

Go ahead, let's do it now—what have you chosen as an "and/or" reality? Now consider the "why" you believe you can't have both. I'll let you in on a secret: Unless it defies the basic laws of the Universe, those rules are in your head. Take that same situation for a moment and just ask yourself *"why not?"* When you're honest with yourself, do you have really valid reasons for your beliefs or actions surrounding it, or was some old programming playing a role? You can have it all; you can live in an *"all* reality" rather than in an "and / or mentality."

Prayer to the Universe

I feel so much joy when I believe that I can have it all and spare myself from choices between two great options. Even if I have to give up another, I will not consider losing something because the choices I make come from my authentic self. There is no pain or sacrifice because my choice was authentic. I embrace abundance and celebrate

my power to have all that can serve me well.

Chapter 27: Authentic Manifestation

I was in full manifestation mode while writing this book. It actually only took about three months to write, and I was juggling a lot of others things. It's a great reminder that amazing things can happen with little time when we are vibrating on our authentic frequency.

Acquiring the things we want and achieving feats we dream about is not that difficult, as we tend to create it to be in our minds. When we understand how manifestation is a mixture of science and Universal power instead of total woo-woo madness, we can have a deeper and more appreciative understanding of the human experience. The great Tesla said that everything is literally energy. This principle is one of the core concepts of quantum physics. So check out the logic behind my formula: Energy influences our thoughts; thoughts influence our emotions. Emotions produce vibrations. Strong emotions produce strong vibrations. Vibrations, when strong enough, collect in one general area until they create matter. So, in extremely simple terms, vibrations can produce realities and matter. Thoughts can be made manifest. Therefore, thoughts create our physical reality.

Every cell in your body reacts to the quality of your thoughts. They manifest the dominant energy you hold or could be "identified" as. A roomful of people have different emotions, but the dominant one has the power to create. It takes only a pinpoint of light to shine into a dark room… you see what I'm saying here? A country has countless streams of emotions from its people, but the dominant, or collective, energy manifests the overall reality. *You* have countless streams of emotions, but you also have some that show up more often than others, thus creating your overall vibration.

If you spend time thinking about all kinds of negativity, guess what you'll produce? Negative results. On the other hand, if you dwell on positive thoughts, you are bound to create positive results. It is not just thoughts that create, but your dominant energy. You might wonder why you couldn't manifest what you want despite your positive thoughts. Check your dominant energy. Just like water, emotions have levels of purity and clarity. Perhaps you are not committed to your thought intentions, and that is why they do not translate into your dominant emotion. In my 30-Day Authentic Creation and Manifestation program, I call this the subconscious reel. You may consciously desire something, but your subconscious is sending out an opposing thought energy that is in direct contradiction to your conscious desire. Years ago, I may have consciously said I wanted a beautiful relationship and man I could trust, but my subconscious (which never shuts off) was saying, "That means you'll really love him, and then you could risk losing him. It's not safe. Don't do it!" So I couldn't create that man until I aligned my frequencies and made sure my dominant energy was telling the Universe my true desires.

It is science when we say that there's a reaction to every action. In spiritual terms, it is Karma—you reap what you sow. You get what you give back. Life is a boomerang. Now, I don't believe the idea that if you do wrong, you now need to wait for wrong to be done unto you. I believe when you raise your frequency and align with your authentic self, karma doesn't have to exist, but you will certainly always get what you give out to the Universe on a consistent basis, so by choosing your

authentic and positive frequency, you naturally remove the negative or

scary idea of consequences with Karma.

So, start going over the dominant emotions you have in the

different compartments of your life. Be honest with yourself. Your

intention or thoughts should be really rooted to the core of your

authentic self so that it has the power to generate your dominant

emotion. Think of a generator. When the dynamo—your

thoughts—starts revolving really intensely fast, it starts to create light

effortlessly. The result the dynamo produces is relative to its action.

One vibrant dominant frequency holds on to the intentions and thoughts

that you really want to create. If it is coming from your authentic self, it

will manifest itself quite quickly, as you're making yourself a straight

shot for all your desires by vibrating so high.

Make your whole being one spiritual generator that produces

dominant emotions rooted in love, happiness, and peace. There are

happy billionaires as much as unhappy ones. Their thoughts did, in fact, manifest money, and they thought it would make them happy. But for those who turned out sad and unhappy, they created it from a misalignment. It was not money they wanted but something more fulfilling. Remember, we are *all* manifesters of our reality. It's just a matter of understanding what you're actually asking the Universe for in the first place. The important thing is to examine the value of what you want to create: Will it serve my purpose and desires in the highest good of all?

Prayer to the Universe

I hold the power to create and manifest what I want in life. Yet, I have taken for granted this power and allowed myself to play small. But now, I embrace my power to manifest. I will create love, abundance, and happiness for myself and for the world that I want to serve.

Chapter 28: Rewiring for Love

The mind is a field where thoughts can at times battle for dominance. In this chapter, I will teach you a simple but powerful technique for how to rewire your mind so that positivity dominates your thoughts.

Wired to Guilt

Since we were children, we were programmed by so many conflicting belief systems. These beliefs have flooded our minds for so long that it has become an entangled ball of yarn. We don't know what's right anymore. We start living in the gray area in parts of our lives. Even when we try to, we can't seem to connect the dots. Because of these mental entanglements, somewhere along the way we begin to believe that we are not worthy, that we should not trust our intuition, that we should feel guilt because of this and that. Our minds were wired to catch the smallest negative thought and shut out whatever positivity that is within and outside of us. Sadly, we are prone to looking for dangers and risks, to see what could go wrong and not what could go right. Other people's belief systems can train us to hold back and withhold our passion for living.

The simplest technique you can use whenever negative talk pops up is to replace it with two positive thoughts. It can be hard to see the benefit at first, but it helps shift the energy. Make sure you also live consciously in those moments when you're aware those thoughts are surfacing. Ask yourself, "Why are they showing up?" Are these thoughts choices or ultimate realities? Are they even valid? These negative thoughts could be anything, such as saying to yourself that you were stupid for forgetting something, or that all people are hurtful. Replace, or at least process, each thought as soon as they pop up.

Try this: At the end of each day before sleeping, get a journal and jot down your answers to these questions: What did I do right today? Who did I help today? What am I proud of? Practice this and dedicate a moment each night for this ritual. Give gratitude to yourself and others. It takes one shift in your perception to move your frequency to authenticity.

Prayer to the Universe

I open myself to all the positive, great, awesome, and amazing things around me. I let go of all negativity and mental trash that's been rotting deep inside of me. I am not only rewiring my mind but my whole being. Behold, I am a new person!

Chapter 29: Detachment

I am the queen of looking and living in the future. Constantly figuring out what next month will be like, or next year even. It's a great skill to have if done in a healthy way, but I didn't use it as such. I used it to create a false sense of certainty in my life. It robbed me of my experiences in the *now*.

Detachment grants us peace of mind because it operates in the space of truth and authenticity. Attachment really does lead to suffering. But that doesn't mean you can't love anything or shouldn't connect to anything in life—that's not the case at all! What we should be detached from are expectations or outcomes. Everything in this world changes, therefore expectations when it comes to situations may not always be met as you plan them out, so going with the flow of life with faith in your heart is so much more rewarding and far less disappointing. I promise it will always turn out beautifully when you choose to see it, regardless.

The Attic

Imagine that you have lost a very expensive ring in a crowded attic. There are tons of old things piled on top of each other. Those things have no more value, but you keep them for the sake of keeping them. Imagine the cobwebs and the dust that have settled in there.

So, what do you do to find your expensive ring?

The best way is to remove all the stuff until the entire attic is empty.

This imagery is a good way to make you understand detachment. Your expensive ring is the authentic self you are searching for. Detachment is the act of removing the useless stuff inside so that you can find your authentic self.

Detachment

Detachment creates a space inside of us. Detachment is not only for physical things but for emotions, belief systems, feelings and expectations of people that do not serve our purpose. Detachment enables us to expand ourselves. Now it's important to remember, when you remove something it must be replaced, or it will fill back up with the same substance that was there previously.

When you come to think about it, there's absolutely no reason to attach ourselves to anything, whether internal or external. Nothing is permanent. Everything changes. People can change overnight. Promises could be broken on the same token they were made. Does that immediately give you an anxious feeling? You definitely need to work on detachment if so.

With detachment, we are able to enjoy life each moment because we have no expectations and we are aware that all things are temporary. So enjoy the ride when it's high, and be thankful for the lessons learned when it's low.

And, when nothing seems to be going your way, say: "This too shall pass."

Look at anything you may be attached to that feels it needs to go. You should be reading this chapter on the 29th day you've spent with me, and if you've taken this book as seriously as I trust you have, I know your intuition is speaking loud lately. So trust it. Whatever is coming up that you may need to be detached from, perhaps not released, but emotionally or energetically detached from, trust it.

Ground yourself and begin removing the clutter in whatever way feels intuitively true to you.

Prayer to the Universe

In the highest good of all, I remove all that no longer should be attached to me. I pray for the clarity to know what it is, and the bravery to remove it regardless of what I find. I trust in myself, and in God/Universe, so that I may continue to experience all that is for me. Please remove all I do not need in my highest version, and bring me all that I need.

Chapter 30: Selling Your Frequency/Energy

Here we are. Today marks 30 days together. Yes, even as you read this now, I know my spirit was with you every day that you read these words. Carrying you when you needed it, applauding all the shifts you chose. You could have cowered away, not heard the words, not felt the energy I was pouring in, but I trust instead that you chose what may have been harder. You accepted and allowed what lessons, messages, and words were meant for you.

And if for some reason you haven't yet, and you feel you don't "deserve" the praise above, that's okay, too. I also trust that you're going to flip back to day 1 and show yourself love and patience and start right over. Sometimes I like to read something over and over until I can almost rehearse it. I remember when I was living in my little condo in Florida, miserable as can be, I took just two weeks out and listened to a recording from the great Earl Nightingale over and over and over again. It took only a few weeks, and my life began to change so drastically because I had programmed his positive and truthful words into me, and I began to portray that reality more so than my own. It was a game changer for me.

If you find yourself ever lost in a situation, consider what daily lesson you need and rest assured that when you follow them, you'll be moving in the right direction to get back into a state of flow again. This is not called the "human experience" by chance. It is just that, an experience—a beautiful and intricate one that is far more vast and expansive than we typically give credit for on a daily basis.

I'm so proud of you for spending the past 30 days with this book, and what I hope you felt, with me, in spirit. I trust that you will continue to move forward in this world with magic and that you will share the lessons, and perhaps the entire book, with your loved ones.

Cheers to your must authentic life lived through love.

And in case no one has told you today,

I love you.

Made in the USA
Middletown, DE
15 April 2019